Spanish

Learn Spanish For Beginners Including Spanish Grammar, Spanish Short Stories and 1000+ Spanish Phrases

Contents

Part 1: Spanish

An Essential Guide to Spanish Language Learning

Introduction (*introducción*)

¡Buenos días!

Spanish is the official language of 20 countries and around 400 million people speak it. Not only is it one of the most spoken languages in the world, but Spanish is also one of the most studied… by you and many others!

If you've never studied Spanish before or if you've studied it but you need to go back to the basics to get better, this handbook will provide you with everything you need, especially if you are planning on traveling to Latin America or Spain!

Not only will we give you the basic grammar rules, but also many fun exercises for you to practice. Don't be afraid, Spanish is easier than it seems!

Even if improvising a sign language is always an option, communicating with locals the right way will allow you to learn Spanish appropriately, so it can become a proper asset for your work, studies, and social life.

And it can really be an asset, since so many people speak and study this language nowadays, even in the corporate and academic worlds. On top of that, having friends in Latin America or Spain is something you'll never regret if you love traveling.

Once you're fluent in Spanish, you'll find a door to a whole new cultural world. For example, you'll be able to read books in Spanish that are not yet translated to your language, or you'll be able to pop into any cinema in Latin America and enjoy a good local movie without subtitles.

Because learning a language is a full experience, we encourage you to use this book but also to travel, to immerse yourself in the Spanish-speaking cultures, to read fiction and newspapers in Spanish, to watch films, to eat Latin American and Spanish food and learn the recipes, to make Spanish-speaking friends and, most important, to enjoy all this.

We hope you have fun using this book!

¡Buena suerte!

Chapter 1 – Pronunciation (*pronunciación*)

Spanish pronunciation is really simple in comparison to other languages. The Spanish alphabet contains 27 letters, most of which are pronounced in only one way. Nonetheless, there are a few exceptions, which we will cover in this section.

Vowels (*vocales*)

Letter *a* is always pronounced as the *a* in *apricot*. You will find this sound in words like *casa* (*house*).

Letter *e* is always pronounced as the e in elephant. You will find this sound in words like *verde* (*green*).

Letter *i* always sounds like the *i* in *intelligence* or the *ee* in *meet* (when it's stressed). You can find this sound in words like *inglés* (*English*), *argentino* (*Argentinian*) or *salir* (*to go out*).

Letter *o* always sounds like the *o* in *tongue*. You can find this sound in words like *tomate* (*tomato*) and *vaso* (*glass*).

Letter *u* always sounds like the *oo* in *pool* or like English *w* in *water*. You can find this sound in words like *luna* (*moon*) and *usar* (*to use*).

Consonants (*consonantes*)

Letter *b* in Spanish is similar to letter *b* in English, but while in English it sounds harder when it's in the beginning of a word (as in *beautiful*), in Spanish it's always a soft sound (as in *cabin*). You will find it in words like *bebé* (*baby*).

Letter *c* in Spanish can have three sounds:

The first is like the *c* in *cut*. Letter *c* always sounds like this when it comes before letters *a*, *o*, *u* and consonants (except *h*), as in words like *cama* (*bed*), *cosa* (*thing*), *cuento* (*tale*) and *acto* (*act*).

The second *c* sound is the same as the *s* sound. It sounds like this when it comes before letters *e* and *i*, as in *cerilla* (*match*) or *cien* (*a hundred*).

The third sound is only possible when *c* comes before *h*, just as it happens in English. The combination of *c* and *h* sounds like the *ch* in *change*. You will find it in words like *colchón* (*mattress*).

Letter *d* in Spanish is similar to *d* in English (as in *daisy*), but slightly softer. You can find it in words such as *dedo* (*finger*).

Letter *f* in Spanish sounds like *f* in English, in words such as *fish*. You will find this sound in Spanish words like *feliz* (*happy*).

Letter *g* in Spanish can have two different sounds:

When it comes before letters *a*, *o*, *u* and consonants, it sounds like a soft version of the English *g* sound in *green*. You can find this sound in words like *gato* (*cat*), *gota* (*drop*), *gusto* (*taste*) and *gracias* (*thanks*). You also get this sound when you have the combination of letters *gue* and *gui*. In these cases, the *u* is not pronounced, just as it happens in English in *guest* or *guilty*. You can find this sound in Spanish in words such as *guerra* (*war*) and *guitarra* (*guitar*). The *u* is only pronounced when there's a dieresis (two dots) on top of it, as in *pingüino* (*penguin*) or *antigüedad* (*antique*), but this is not very common.

The second *g* sound in Spanish is similar to the *h* sound in English word *helicopter*. You can find this sound when *g* comes before letters *e* and *i*, as in *gente* (*people*) or *girasol* (*sunflower*).

Letter *h* in Spanish is mute. You will normally find it at the beginning of words, such as *hielo* (*ice*) or *huevo* (*egg*), but it can also be in the middle, as in *almohada* (*pillow*). The only situation where *h* has a sound is in combination with *c*, as in *chocolate* (*chocolate*).

Letter *j* in Spanish sounds like the Spanish *g* before letters *e* and *i*. This means it sounds similar to English *h* in words like *heaven*. You can find this letter in words such as *jamón* (*ham*), *jefe* (*boss*) and *joven* (*young*).

Letter *k* is not used in many words in Spanish, but you can find it in some like *kilo* (*kilo*) and *kiosco* (*kiosk*). The sound is the same as the sound of letter *c* when it comes before letters *a*, *o*, *u* and consonants, as in *cantar* (*to sing*).

Letter *l* in Spanish sounds exactly as letter *l* in English. You can find it in words such as *limón* (*lemon*) or *loco* (*crazy*). However, when two *l* are put together, the sound changes. The *ll* sounds different in different Latin American countries and in Spain. It's pronounced like the Spanish *i*, like the combination *li*, like the English *y* in *yellow*, like the *j* in *jello* or like the *sh* in *show*.

Letter *m* in Spanish always sounds like the *m* in English, as in *monster*. You can find this letter in words like *miedo* (*fear*) or *mejor* (*better*).

Letter *n* in Spanish always sounds like the *n* in English, as in *nonsense*. You can find this letter in words like *nunca* (*never*) or *nada* (*nothing*).

Letter *ñ* sounds like the combination of letters *ni*, as in *nibble*. You can find this letter in words as *niño* (*kid*), where the *ni* and the *ñ* sound exactly the same. Other words with letter *ñ* are *contraseña* (*password*), *señal* (*signal*) and *dueño* (*owner*).

Letter *p* in Spanish sounds softer than the English *p*. It is actually more similar to the English *b* in *because*. You can find this sound in words like *perro* (*dog*) or *rápido* (*fast*).

Letter *q* is only used in Spanish in the combinations *que* and *qui*. In these cases, the *u* is silent and the *q* sounds like *c* when it comes before letters *a*, *o*, *u* and consonants, as in *coco* (*coconut*). You can find letter *q* in words like *queso* (*cheese*) and *quizás* (*maybe*).

Letter *r* has two different sounds in Spanish:

> The strong *r* sound is very difficult to non-Spanish speakers, so if you want to roll your *r* like a local, you need to try to place your tongue in the front of your palate, right behind your teeth, and try to make air pass through until it sounds like a starting engine. You'll need this sound for words that start with *r*, like *rata* (*rat*), and for words that have a double *r*, like *perro* (*dog*).

> The soft *r* is easier, and it sounds like the American sound for *t* in *water*. You'll use the soft *r* in words like *cara* (*face*).

Letter *s* always sounds like the *s* in *snake*. You'll use this sound in words like *silla* (*chair*) or *Sol* (*sun*).

Letter *t* sounds stronger than American *t* and a little bit softer than British *t*. You'll use this sound in words like *tomate* (*tomato*) and *techo* (*roof*).

Letter *v* sounds similar to English *v*, maybe a little bit softer and sometimes not really different to *b*. You'll find this sound in words like *vaca* (*cow*) and *vaso* (*glass*).

Letter *w* is not really common in Spanish. It is only used in word with a foreign origin, like those that come from English. It is pronounced like the English *w* and you'll find it in words like *kiwi* and *show*, which mean the same as in English.

Letter *x* is also not really common in Spanish, but it used more than *k* and *w*. It sounds like a strong *c* and an *s* put together, just like in English. You'll use it in words like *taxi* (*taxi*) and *conexión* (*connection*).

Letter *y* has two different sounds:

> It sounds like Spanish *i* (like the *i* in *intelligence* or the *ee* in *meet*) in words like *y* (*and*) or *hoy* (*today*).

> It can sound like Spanish *ll* and also sounds different in different Latin American countries and in Spain: it's pronounced like the Spanish *i*, like the English *y* in *yellow,* the *j* in *jello,* or the *sh* in *show.* You'll find it in really common words like *yo* (*I*) and *ya* (*now*).

Letter *z* is pronounced, in some countries, like an *s*; but in some others, like Spain, it sounds similar to the *th* in *with* or *throne.* You'll use the *z* in words like *cazar* (*to hunt*) and *zorro* (*fox*).

Accentuation (*acentuación*)

As you've probably noticed before, in Spanish we can put a little mark on top of the vowels to accentuate them: *á, é, í, ó, ú.* In Spanish, this means you have to have to stress (accentuate) the word where the mark (the *tilde*) is.

It's not the same to say *estas* (*these*) than to say *estás* (*you are*). In the first case, you stress the first syllable and, in the second case, you stress the final syllable.

The basic rules for accentuating might sound a bit complicated now, but they're actually simpler than they seem. You don't need to learn these by heart to understand or to speak Spanish, but they are useful if you want to learn how to write properly.

1- If the word is stressed in the last syllable, you have to write the *tilde* when it ends in a vowel, an *s* or an *n*: *estás* (*you are*), *colibrí* (*hummingbird*), *perdió* (*he lost*), *colchón* (*mattress*). If they end in any other letter, they are still stressed in the last syllable, but you don't have to write the *tilde*: *borrar* (*to erase*), *motor* (*engine*), *feliz* (*happy*).

2- If the word is stressed in the second to last syllable, you have to write the *tilde* when it ends in any letter *but* a vowel, an *s* or an *n*: *árbol* (*tree*), *lápiz* (*pencil*), *útil* (*useful*). If they end in a vowel, an *s* or an *n*, these words are still stressed in the second to last syllable, but you don't have to write the *tilde*: *alegre* (*cheerful*), *amarillo* (*yellow*), *beso* (*kiss*).

3- If the word is stressed in any syllable before the second to last, it always has to have a *tilde*: *murciélago* (*bat*), *física* (*physics*), *gramática* (*grammar*), *matemáticas* (*math*).

There are a few **exceptions**.

Adverbs that end in *-mente* (*-ly*) don't always follow the third rule. They keep the accentuation of the original word, as if the *-mente* suffix weren't there, even though they're alway stressed in the second to last syllable: *claramente* (*clearly*), *velozmente* (*quickly*), *últimamente* (*lately*).

Another exception is that vowels *i* and *u* always have to carry a *tilde* when they're stressed and come before or after vowels *a, e* or *o*: *raíz* (*root*), *país* (*country*), *baúl* (*trunk*), *freír* (*to fry*), *sandía* (*watermelon*), *frío* (*cold*).

Chapter 2 – Pronouns (*pronombres*)

Personal pronouns (*pronombres personales*)

I - yo

you - tú/vos/usted

he - él

she - ella

we - nosotros

you - ustedes/vosotros

they - ellos/ellas

In Spain and most of Latin America, the pronoun used for singular *you* is *tú*, but in some places (like Argentina, Uruguay, Paraguay and some regions of Bolivia, Colombia and other Latin American countries) the pronoun *vos* is used instead.

This pronoun uses a slightly different conjugation for most verbs. If you want to be understood in every Spanish-speaking country, though, learning the pronoun *tú* is more than enough.

In any case, here are some major differences in some important irregular and regular verbs:

To be (*ser*): you are - tú eres / vos sos

To be (*estar*): you are - tú estás / vos estás

To have (*tener*): you have - tú tienes / vos tenés

To live (*vivir*): you live - tú vives / vos vivís

To say (*decir*): you say - tú dices / vos decís

To go (*ir*): you go - tú vas / vos vas

To do (*hacer*): you do - tú haces / vos hacés

To love (*amar*): you love - tú amas / vos amás

Usted is the formal *you*. In some countries, it is more used than in others, but it is generally recommended when talking to people you don't know, older people and important people. *Usted* is conjugated differently than *tú* or *vos*. It's really simple to use, because it uses the same conjugation as *él* (*he*) or *ella* (*she*). Examples:

To be (*ser*)

he/she is - él/ella es

you are - usted es

To be (*estar*)

he/she is - él/ella está

you are - usted está

To have (*tener*)

he/she has - él/ella tiene

you have - usted tiene

To live (*vivir*)

he/she lives - él/ella vive

you live - usted vive

When it comes to plural *you* (when there's more than one person), in most Latin American countries the pronoun used is *ustedes*. In Spain, they normally use *vosotros* instead. *Ustedes* is really easy to conjugate: it always uses the same conjugation as *ellos/ellas* (*they*). Examples:

To be (*ser*)

they are - ellos/ellas son

you are - ustedes son / vosotros sois

To be (*estar*)

they are - ellos/ellas están

you are - ustedes están / vosotros estáis

To have (*tener*)

they have - ellos/ellas tienen

you have - ustedes tienen / vosotros tenéis

To live (*vivir*)

they live - ellos/ellas viven

you live - ustedes viven / vosotros vivís

Possessive pronouns

In Spanish we have two kinds of possessive pronouns (*mi libro; el libro es **mío***), just like in English (***my** book; the book is **mine***). The only big difference is that we have plural possessive pronouns for when we're talking about more than one possession (*mis libros; los libros son **míos***). These are the *posesivos antepuestos*, or *átonos*, that we put before the possession:

my - mi

your - tu

his/her - su

our - nuestro/nuestra

your - su/vuestro/vuestra

their - su

And these are their plurals:

my - mis

your - tus

his/her - sus

our - nuestros/nuestras

your - sus/vuestros/vuestras

their - sus

Examples

My house is around the corner - **Mi** casa está a la vuelta de la esquina

My friends are always there for me - **Mis** amigos están siempre ahí para mí

May I borrow **your** notebook? - ¿Me prestas **tu** cuaderno?

May I borrow **your** notes? - ¿Me prestas **tus** apuntes?

I love **her** hair – Me encanta **su** cabello

I don't care about **her** problemas - No me interesan **sus** problemas

You are always welcome in **our** home - Siempre serás bienvenido en **nuestro** hogar

You'll always be in **our** thoughts - Siempre estarás en **nuestros** pensamientos

Your service improves every day - **Vuestro** servicio mejora todos los días

Your clients never complain - **Vuestros** clientes jamás se quejan

Their problem is **their** lack of training - **Su** problema es la falta de entrenamiento

I love their uniforms! - ¡Me encantan **sus** uniformes!

The second kind of possessive pronouns are the *posesivos pospuestos*, or *tónicos*.

mine - mío/mía

yours - tuyo/tuya

his/hers - suyo/suya

ours - nuestro/nuestra

yours - suyo/suya/vuestro/vuestra

theirs - suyo/suya

And these are their plurals:

mine - míos/mías

yours - tuyos/tuyas

his/hers - suyos/suyas

ours - nuestros/nuestras

yours - suyos/suyas/vuestros/vuestras

theirs - suyos/suyas

Examples

The car is **mine** - El auto es **mío**

The ideas are **mine** - Las ideas son **mías**

The world is **yours** - El mundo es **tuyo**

Are these trousers **yours**? - ¿Estos pantalones son **tuyos**?

The song wasn't **hers** - La canción no era **suya**

Benefits are **his** - Los beneficios son **suyos**

The fault is **ours** - La culpa es **nuestra**

Responsibilities are **ours** - Las responsabilidades son **nuestras**

The result is **yours** - El resultado es **vuestro**

Leftovers are **yours** - Las sobras son **vuestras**

Their love is only **theirs** - Su amor es **suyo**

The children are **theirs** - Los hijos son **suyos**

Demonstrative pronouns

While in English you have *this* and *that*, in Spanish we have three demonstrative pronouns: *este, ese* and *aquel*, and their feminine forms and plurals.

Este is used to talk about a noun that is close to the speaker:

this pencil - **este** lápiz

this mug - **esta** taza

these objects - **estos** objetos

these spoons - **estas** cucharas

Ese is used to talk about something not very close to the speaker (though it may be close to the listener):

that problem - **ese** problema

that house - **esa** casa

those years - **esos** años

those oranges - **esas** naranjas

Aquel is used to replace something far from both the speaker and the listener:

that day - **aquel** día

that woman - **aquella** mujer

those students - **aquellos** estudiantes

those girls - **aquellas** niñas

Relative pronouns

The use of relative pronouns in Spanish is not very different from English. While in English you use *that, which, where, when, who* and *whom*, in Spanish we use *que, quien, cuando* and *donde*. *Que* can be always used, while *quien* is only used for people.

He gave you money **that** was mine - Él te dio dinero **que** era mío

The woman **who** did it is over there - La mujer **que** lo hizo está allí

He's the brother with **whom** I grew up - Él es el hermano con **quien** crecí

That's the town **where** I was born - Ese es el pueblo **donde** nací

I remember the morning **when** I met you - Recuerdo la mañana **cuando** te conocí

You can also use the constructions *el que* and *el cual*, and their feminine forms and plurals:

The hotel **where** I stayed is beautiful - El hotel en **el que** me hospedé es hermoso

I have a car, **which** is very old and needs repairs- Tengo un auto, **el cual** es muy viejo y necesita arreglos

The morning **when** I met you was sunny - La mañana en **la que** te conocí era soleada

I have tools, **which** I might lend you some day - Tengo herramientas, **las cuales** quizá te preste algún día

Interrogative pronouns

Just as in English, when we ask questions we often start with *what (qué), who (quién), where (dónde), when (cuándo), how (cómo)* and *how much (cuánto/cuánta/cuántos/cuántas).* Examples:

What did she say? - ¿**Qué** dijo?

Who's coming to dinner? - ¿**Quién** viene a cenar?

Where should I leave my shoes? - ¿**Dónde** debo dejar mis zapatos?

How are we going to recognize each other? - ¿**Cómo** vamos a reconocernos?

How many girlfriends do you have? - ¿**Cuántas** novias tienes?

Just like in English, you can also use these interrogative pronouns in affirmative sentences.

He asked **what** Raquel had said - Me preguntó **qué** dijo Raquel

She asked **who** was coming to dinner - Me preguntó **quién** venía a cenar

I asked **where** should I leave my shoes - Pregunté **dónde** debía dejar los zapatos

I asked **how** we were going to recognize each other - Pregunté **cómo** nos íbamos a reconocer

I asked him **how many** girlfriends he has - Le pregunté **cuántas** novias tiene

Indefinite pronouns

someone - alguien

something - algo

one - alguno/alguna/uno/una

some - algunos/algunas/unos/unas

any - cualquier/cualquiera

much/many - mucho/mucha/muchos/muchas

nothing - nada

nobody - nadie

no one - ninguno/ninguna

another one / other - otro/otra/otros/otras

a few / little / a little bit - poco/poca/pocos/pocas

every / everything - todo/toda/todos/todas

Examples

Can **someone** help me? - ¿**Alguien** puede ayudarme?

I have **something** to tell you - Tengo **algo** que decirte

One of us has to go - **Alguno** de nosotros debe ir

I have **some** ideas - Tengo **algunas** ideas

Any of them is OK - **Cualquiera** de ellos está bien

I have **many** problems - Tengo **muchos** problemas

I have **nothing** to lose - No tengo **nada** que perder

Nobody's arguing with you - **Nadie** está discutiendo contigo

No one showed up - **Ninguno** asistió

I have **other** things to do - Tengo **otras** cosas que hacer

I have **little** patience - Tengo **poca** paciencia

I want to take **every** chance there is - Quiero tomar **todas** las oportunidades que haya

Direct object pronouns (*pronombres de objeto directo*)

A direct object pronoun replaces a direct object, which is a noun that directly receives the action of a verb in a sentence.

For example, we can say *Lancé la bola* (*I threw the ball*), but we can also say *La lancé* (*I threw it*).

These are the direct object pronouns:

me - me

you - te

it/him/her - lo/la

us - nos

you - los/las/os

them - los/las

Examples

They called **her** to congratulate **her** - **La** llamaron para felicitar**la**

They called **him** to congratulate **him** - **Lo** llamaron para felicitar**lo**

We need the bags, bring **them**! - Necesitamos las bolsas, ¡trae**las**!

Indirect object pronouns (*pronombres de objeto indirecto*)

An indirect object pronoun tells you to whom or for whom something is done. These are sometimes confusing, because they are similar to the direct object pronouns, but with time and practice you can get them right.

If we say *Ana compró un libro a José* (*Ana bought a book to/for José*), we can also say *Ana le compró un libro* (*Ana bought him a book*).

to/for me - me

to/for you - te

to/for him/her/it - le

to/for us - nos

to/for you - les/os

to/for them - les

Examples

They asked **me** a favor - **Me** pidieron un favor

I will give **you** a surprise - **Te** daré una sorpresa

I wish they give **us** a job - Ojalá **nos** den un empleo

Did they give **you** the address? - ¿**Os** dieron la dirección?

Chapter 3 – Basic verbs (*verbos básicos*)

All verbs in Spanish end in *-ar*, *-er* or *-ir*. Regular verbs that end in the same way follow the same rules of conjugation, but there are also irregular verbs, some of which are very important, like verbs *ser* and *estar* (both of which translate as *to be*).

Basic regular verbs ending in -ar

Regular verbs that end in *-ar* always follow the same structure and add the same letters after the root of the verb, as in the following example. For the verb *amar* (*to love*), the root is *am-*.

To love (*amar*)

yo am**o**

tú am**as** / vos am**ás** / usted am**a**

él/ella am**a**

nosotros am**amos**

ustedes am**an** / vosotros am**áis**

ellos/ellas am**an**

You can practice conjugating the following regular Spanish verbs ending in *-ar*: *caminar* (*to walk*), *extrañar* (*to miss*), *hablar* (*to talk*).

Basic regular verbs ending in -er

Regular verbs that end in *-er* also follow the same structure and add the same letters after the root of the verb, as in the following example. For the verb *temer* (*to fear*), the root is *tem-*.

To fear (*temer*)

yo tem**o**

tú tem**es** / vos tem**és** / usted tem**e**

él/ella tem**e**

nosotros tem**emos**

ustedes tem**en** / vosotros tem**éis**

ellos/ellas tem**en**

You can practice conjugating the following regular Spanish verbs ending in *-er*: *beber* (*to drink*), *creer* (*to believe*), *vender* (*to sell*).

Basic regular verbs ending in -ir

Regular verbs that end in *-ir* also follow the same structure and add the same letters after the root of the verb, as in the following example. For the verb *vivir* (*to live*), the root is *viv-*.

To live (*vivir*)

yo viv**o**

tú viv**es** / vos viv**ís** / usted viv**e**

él/ella viv**e**

nosotros viv**imos**

ustedes viv**en** / vosotros viv**ís**

ellos/ellas viv**en**

You can practice conjugating the following regular Spanish verbs ending in *-ir*: *partir* (*to leave*), *abrir* (*to open*), *escribir* (*to write*).

To be and to be (*ser y estar*)

Present tense conjugation of verb to be (*ser*)

yo **soy**

tú **eres** / vos **sos** / usted **es**

él/ella **es**

nosotros **somos**

ustedes **son** / vosotros **sois**

ellos/ellas **son**

Present tense conjugation of verb to be (*estar*)

yo **estoy**

tú **estás** / vos **estás** / usted **está**

él/ella **está**

nosotros **estamos**

ustedes **están** / vosotros **estáis**

ellos/ellas **están**

The difference with verbs *ser* and *estar* is that *ser* normally refers to a permanent state, while *estar* is more of a passing state. Here are some examples in sentences:

I am Sandra - **Soy** Sandra

I am tired - **Estoy** cansado

You are an idiot - **Eres** un idiota

You are in trouble - **Estás** en problemas

He is a doctor - Él **es** médico

He is running a marathon - Él **está** corriendo una maratón

We are husband and wife - **Somos** marido y mujer

We are in love - **Estamos** enamorados

You are the best - **Sois** los mejores

You are hiding something - **Estáis** ocultando algo

They are losers - **Son** perdedores

They are coming! - ¡**Están** viniendo!

Other irregular verbs

To have (*tener*)

yo **tengo**

tú **tienes** / vos **tenés** / usted **tiene**

él/ella **tiene**

nosotros **tenemos**

ustedes **tienen** / vosotros **tenéis**

ellos/ellas **tienen**

<u>To say</u> (*decir*)

yo **digo**

tú **dices** / vos **decís** / usted **dice**

él/ella **dice**

nosotros **decimos**

ustedes **dicen** / vosotros **decís**

ellos/ellas **dicen**

<u>To go</u> (*ir*)

yo **voy**

tú **vas** / vos **vas** / usted **va**

él/ella **va**

nosotros **vamos**

ustedes **van** / vosotros **vais**

ellos/ellas **van**

<u>To do</u> (*hacer*)

yo **hago**

tú **haces** / vos **hacés** / usted **hace**

él/ella **hace**

nosotros **hacemos**

ustedes **hacen** / vosotros **hacéis**

ellos/ellas **hacen**

<u>Can</u> (*poder*)

yo **puedo**

tú **puedes** / vos **podés** / usted **puede**

él/ella **puede**

nosotros **podemos**

ustedes **pueden** / vosotros **podéis**

ellos/ellas **pueden**

<u>To see (*ver*)</u>

yo **veo**

tú **ves** / vos **ves** / usted **ve**

él/ella **ve**

nosotros **vemos**

ustedes **ven** / vosotros **veis**

ellos/ellas **ven**

<u>To give (*dar*)</u>

yo **doy**

tú **das** / vos **das** / usted **da**

él/ella **da**

nosotros **damos**

ustedes **dan** / vosotros **dais**

ellos/ellas **dan**

<u>To want (*querer*)</u>

yo **quiero**

tú **quieres** / vos **querés** / usted **quiere**

él/ella **quiere**

nosotros **queremos**

ustedes **quieren** / vosotros **queréis**

ellos/ellas **quieren**

Exercises

Note that, in Spanish, you don't need to always write the pronoun before the verb, as you do in English. For example, in English you have to say "*I am happy*", but can't just say "*Am happy*". In Spanish, instead, you can say both "*Yo estoy feliz*" or simply "*Estoy feliz*". Normally, you don't say the pronoun unless you want to emphasise it, as in "*Él no es el asesino, yo soy el asesino*" ("*He's not the killer, I am the killer*").

In the following exercises, you have to complete either the conjugated verb or the corresponding pronoun:

I am Ana´s best friend - … soy la mejor amiga de Ana

You are a great boss - Usted ... un gran jefe

He is a very smart boy - Él ... un muchacho muy inteligente

We are the best - .... los mejores

You guys are always fighting - Ustedes .... siempre peleando

They are the greatest scientists in their generation - .... son las mejores científicas de su generación

I'm tired - .... cansado

You are prettier each day - .... más lindo cada día

She's sad - .... está triste

We are in danger - .... en peligro

You are crazy - Vosotros .... locos

They are coming - .... están viniendo

I'm cold - .... frío

Do you have a lighter? - ¿.......... un encendedor?

He's afraid - .... miedo

We have what it takes - Nosotros .... lo necesario

I'm OK, but you always have a problem - Yo estoy bien, pero .... tienen siempre algún problema

They have a secret - Ellas .... un secreto

I live alone - .... solo

We live two blocks away - .... a dos cuadras

You say she's lying? - ¿.......... que ella está mintiendo?

They say it's too late - Ellos .... que es demasiado tarde

I'm going to ask you to leave - .... a pedirte que te marches

Let's go dancing! - ¡............. a bailar!

I do what I can - .... lo que puedo

You do the right thing - .... hace lo correcto

We do everything! - ¡Nosotros .... todo!

I love you - Te ....

We love Peruvian food - .... la comida peruana

I can't go - No .... ir

He sees what's going on - Él .... lo que sucede

I give you everything I have - Yo te .... todo lo que tengo

We give our lives for art - .... nuestras vidas por el arte

I want to eat something spicy - .... comer algo picante

Do you want to dance with me? - ¿............ bailar conmigo?

They want to travel - Ellas .... viajar

Chapter 4 – Basic vocabulary (vocabulario *básico*)

In this chapter we are going to introduce you to some basic words you are definitely going to need to know if you want to learn Spanish.

Hello and goodbye (*hola y chau*)

Hello - Hola

How are you? - ¿Cómo estás/está? (informal/formal speech)

I'm well - Estoy bien

Good morning - Buen día

Good afternoon/evening - Buenas tardes

Good night - Buenas noches

Bye - Chau

Goodbye - Adiós

See you later - Hasta luego

Have a nice day - Tenga un buen día

Have a good weekend! - ¡Buen fin de semana!

Take care - Cuídate

You too - Igualmente

See you - Nos vemos

Introductions (*presentaciones*)

What is your name? - ¿Cómo te llamas?

My name is… - Mi nombre es…

Where are you from? - ¿De dónde eres?

I'm from… - Yo soy de…

What do you do for work? - ¿En qué trabajas?

I am… - Soy…

Since when are you in…? - ¿Desde cuándo estás en…?

Do you know…? - ¿Conoces…?

Do you want to go …………tomorrow? - ¿Quieres ir a ……………… mañana?

Let's go ……………… tomorrow - Vayamos a ……………….... mañana

When do we meet? - ¿A qué hora nos encontramos?

Do you have free time tomorrow? - ¿Tienes tiempo mañana?

Call me - Llámame

Yes and no (*sí y no*)

yes - sí

no - no

of course - claro

of course not - claro que no

absolutely - absolutamente

not at all - para nada

for sure - por supuesto

Politeness (*cortesía*)

please - por favor

thanks - gracias

I'm sorry - lo siento

excuse me - disculpe

sorry - perdón

I am sorry - lo lamento

thanks - gracias

thank you very much - muchas gracias

you are welcome - de nada

never mind - no hay por qué

it's fine - está bien

Understanding (*comprensión*)

I understand - Entiendo

I don't understand - No entiendo

Please, speak slowly - Por favor, hable despacio

Could you repeat that, please? - ¿Podría repetir eso, por favor?

Could you write that down, please? - ¿Podría escribir eso, por favor?

Do you speak English? - ¿Habla inglés?

Do you speak Spanish? - ¿Habla español?

Conjunctions (*conjunciones*)

and - y/e

or - o/u

nor - ni

Note that conjunction *e* is only used when we need to say *and* before a word that starts with the letter *i* or with *hi*. Because that would be impossible to pronounce, we use *e*. The same thing happens with conjunction *u*, which is only used when we need to say *or* before a word that starts with letter *o*. Examples:

I have oranges and lemons - Tengo naranjas **y** limones

I have tomatoes and figs - Tengo tomates **e** higos

There are many rivers and islands in that area - Hay muchos ríos **e** islas en esa zona

Do you want tea or coffee? - ¿Quieres té **o** café?

Were they wolves or bears? - ¿Eran lobos **u** osos?

Colours

black - negro

white - blanco

grey - gris

red - rojo

green - verde

blue - azul

yellow - amarillo

orange - naranja

purple - violeta

brown - marrón

Signs

open - abierto

closed - cerrado

entrance - entrada

exit - salida

push - empuje

pull - tire

men - hombres

women - mujeres

occupied - ocupado

vacant - libre

Accomodation

check-in - entrada

check-out - salida

reservation - reserva

vacant room - habitación disponible

to book - reservar

to check in - registrarse

to check out - salir/hacer checkout

to pay the bill - pagar la cuenta

to stay at a hotel - quedarse en un hotel

hotel - hotel

bed and breakfast – alojamiento y desayuno

guesthouse - casa de huéspedes

hostel - hostal

campsite - campamento

single room - habitación simple

double room - habitación doble

twin room - habitación doble con camas separadas

triple room - habitación con tres camas

suite - suite

air conditioning - aire acondicionado

toilet - baño

en-suite bathroom - baño en suite

internet access - acceso a internet

minibar - minibar

safe - caja fuerte

shower - ducha

bar - bar

parking lot - estacionamiento/aparcamiento

corridor - pasillo/corredor

fire escape - salida de incendio

games room - habitación de juegos

gym - gimnasio

laundry service - servicio de lavandería

lift - ascensor

lobby - vestíbulo

reception - recepción

restaurant - restaurante

room service - servicio a la habitación

sauna - sauna

swimming pool - piscina

manager - encargado/a

housekeeper - empleado/a de limpieza

receptionist - recepcionista

doorman - portero

fire alarm - alarma de incendios

laundry - lavandería

room key - llave de la habitación

room number - número de la habitación

wake-up call - llamada de despertador

Clothes

T-shirt - playera/camiseta

shirt - camisa

blouse - blusa

sweatshirt - sudadera

sweater - jersey/suéter

trousers - pantalones

shorts - pantalones cortos

jeans - jeans/vaqueros

suit - traje

sweat pants - pantalón de jogging

dress - vestido

skirt - falda/pollera

miniskirt - minifalda

tie - corbata

tuxedo - esmoquin

vest - chaleco

underwear - ropa interior

socks - calcetines/medias

pajamas - pijama

swimsuit - traje de baño

trunks - bañador

bikini - bikini

coat - abrigo

jacket - chaqueta/saco

poncho - poncho

flip-flops - chanclas/ojotas

sandals - sandalias

loafers - mocasines

sneakers - zapatos deportivos / zapatillas / tenis

heels - tacones/tacos

boots - botas

slippers - pantuflas

cap - gorra

hat - sombrero/gorro

hood - capucha

belt - cinturón

necklace - collar

bracelet - pulsera

watch - reloj

earrings - aretes/pendientes/aritos

ring - anillo

gloves - guantes

scarf - bufanda

sunglasses - gafas de sol / lentes de sol

Languages and demonyms (*idiomas y gentilicios*)

Knowing how to name other languages and people who come from different countries can be useful when meeting people. Remember that, in Spanish, we don't capitalize these words.

These are some common languages, that also work as demonyms. When used as demonyms, they have to match number and gender. For example, two women from Japan are *japonesas*, and three men from Italy are *italianos*.

Spain, Spanish - España, español

England, English - Inglaterra, inglés

Germany, German - Alemania, alemán

France, French - Francia, francés

Italy, Italian - Italia, italiano

The Netherlands, Dutch - Países Bajos, holandés

Portugal, Portuguese - Portugal, portugués

Greece, Greek - Grecia, griego

Russia, Russian - Rusia, ruso

China, Chinese - China, chino

Japan, Japanese - Japón, japonés

The following are not languages, but only demonyms, and their countries:

USA, American - Estados Unidos, estadounidense (never "americano")

Australia, Australian - Australia, australiano

Mexico, Mexican - México, mexicano

Brazil, Brazilian - Brasil, brasileño

Chile, Chilean - Chile, chileno

Argentina, Argentinian - Argentina, argentino

Uruguay, Uruguayan - Uruguay, uruguayo

Cuba, Cuban - Cuba, cubano

Colombia, Colombian - Colombia, colombiano

Venezuela, Venezuelan - Venezuela, venezolano

Peru, Peruvian - Perú, peruano

Bolivia, Bolivian - Bolivia, boliviano

Travelling

How much is a ticket to…? - ¿Cuánto cuesta un pasaje/boleto/billete a…?

One ticket to…, please - Un pasaje a…, por favor

Where does the train/bus to… stop? - ¿Dónde para el tren/bus a…?

When does the train/bus for… leave? - ¿Cuándo parte el tren/bus a…?

Where's the ticket office? - ¿Dónde está la boletería?

What time's the next bus to…? - ¿Cuándo parte el próximo bus a…?

How much is a ticket to…? - ¿Cuánto cuesta el boleto a…?

Which platform do I need to go? - ¿A qué plataforma debo ir?

How often do the buses/trains run to…? - ¿Cuál es la frecuencia de los buses/trenes a…?

The train's running late - El tren tiene retraso

The train's been cancelled - El tren se canceló

When are we arriving to…? - ¿Cuándo llegaremos a…?

I've lost my ticket - Perdí mi billete

This is my stop - Esta es mi parada

single - de ida

return - ida y vuelta

first class - primera clase

train station - estación de trenes

the bus station - estación de buses

airport - aeropuerto

downtown - centro de la ciudad

consulate/embassy - consulado/embajada

map - mapa

street - calle

left - izquierda

right - derecha

straight ahead - derecho

north - Norte

south - Sur

east - Este

west - Oeste

taxi - taxi

How much does it cost to get to…? - ¿Cuánto cuesta ir hasta…?

Are we almost there? - ¿Estamos cerca?

How much is it? - ¿Cuánto es?

What's the address? - ¿Cuál es la dirección?

seat - asiento

luggage rack - portaequipaje

night bus - bus nocturno

passport - pasaporte

holidays - vacaciones

business trip - viaje de negocios

ATM - cajero automático

Do you accept American dollars? - ¿Acepta dólares americanos?

Do you accept British pounds? - ¿Acepta libras esterlinas?

Do you accept euros? - ¿Acepta euros?

Do you accept credit cards? - ¿Acepta tarjeta de crédito?

Can you change money for me? - ¿Puede cambiarme dinero?

Where can I change money? - ¿Dónde puedo cambiar dinero?

What is the exchange rate? - ¿Cuál es la tasa de cambio?

Food

table - mesa

menu - menú

kitchen - cocina

vegetarian - vegetariano/a

I don't eat pork - No como cerdo

I don't eat beef - No como carne de vaca

I only eat kosher food - Solo como comida kosher

breakfast - desayuno

lunch - almuerzo

dinner - cena

dessert - postre

chicken - pollo

beef - res / carne de vaca

fish - pescado

ham - jamón

sausages - salchichas

cheese - queso

eggs - huevos

salad - ensalada

vegetables - vegetales

fruit - fruta

bread - pan

toast - tostadas

pasta - pasta

rice - arroz

beans - frijoles

potatoes - patatas

May I have a glass of…? - ¿Puedo tomar un vaso / una copa de…?

May I have a bottle of…? - ¿Puedo tomar una botella de…?

coffee - café

tea - té

juice - jugo/zumo

water - agua

beer - cerveza

red/white wine - vino tinto/blanco

salt - sal

black pepper - pimienta

butter - mantequilla

Excuse me, waiter? - ¿Disculpe, mesero/camarero/mozo?

It was delicious - Estaba delicioso

The check, please - La cuenta, por favor

food - comida

tip - propina

The weather (*el clima*)

sun/sunshine - sol

rain - lluvia

snow - nieve

hail - granizo

drizzle - llovizna

mist - neblina

fog - niebla

cloud - nube

rainbow - arcoiris

wind - viento

breeze - brisa

thunder - trueno

lightning - relámpago

storm - tormenta

hurricane - huracán

flood - inundación

frost - helada

ice - hielo

windy - ventoso

cloudy - nublado

dry - seco

humid - húmedo

heat - calor

cold - frío

sunny - soleado

rainy - lluvioso

to snow - nevar

to rain - llover

weather forecast - pronóstico del tiempo

temperature - temperatura

Celsius degree - grado centígrado/Celsius

Chapter 5 – Articles (*artículos*)

Definite articles (*artículos definidos*)

Every Spanish noun has a gender, even if it's an object or an abstract concept. This means articles and adjectives must match their gender too. Normally, masculine nouns end in *o* and feminine nouns end in *a*.

In English, there is one definite article: *the*. In Spanish, however, there's one for masculine words and one for feminine words. These are *el* and *la*.

Note that the masculine article *el* is differentiated from personal pronoun *él* with a *tilde*, even though both words are normally pronounced in the same way (sometimes *él* is stressed harder).

<u>Masculine nouns</u>

the phone - el teléfono

the game - el juego

the pen - el bolígrafo

the road - el camino

the notebook - el cuaderno

the book - el libro

the shoe - el zapato

<u>Feminine nouns</u>

the door - la puerta

the chair - la silla

the kitchen - la cocina

the party - la fiesta

the moon - la luna

the table - la mesa

the nose - la nariz

There are also feminine and masculine nouns that end in other letters, or even masculine nouns that end in *a* and feminine nouns that end in *o*, but they're not common:

Masculine nouns

the paper - el papel

the tree - el árbol

the bread - el pan

the coffee - el café

love - el amor

Monday - el lunes

the problem - el problema

the weather - el clima

Feminine nouns

the night -la noche

the skin - la piel

the class - la clase

the snow - la nieve

the picture - la foto

the hand - la mano

the image - la imagen

the people - la gente

There are some feminine words that use the masculine article *el* when they start with a stressed *a*. Even if they use the masculine article, they are still feminine words, which means the adjectives that affect them must be feminine:

the clear water - el agua clara

the bald eagle - el águila calva

the broken wing - el ala rota

the housekeeper - el ama de llaves

There are also plurals for the definite articles: *los* and *las*. You use these when you are talking about plural nouns:

the cats - los gatos

the houses - las casas

the friends - los amigos

the cars - los autos

the whales - las ballenas

the cakes - las tortas

the shoes - los zapatos

the pains - los dolores

the thoughts - los pensamientos

the ideas - las ideas

Contractions (contracciones)

There are two contractions in Spanish. When the definite article *el* comes after prepositions *a* (*to*) or *de* (*from*), they combine to form contractions *al* and *del*. Examples:

I went **to the** market - Fui **al** mercado

I come **from the** market - Vengo **del** mercado

The only exception is when the article is part of a name (you can tell because it will be capitalized):

I will travel **to El** Paso - Voy a viajar **a El** Paso

Juan is **from El** Salvador - Juan es **de El** Salvador

Indefinite articles (*artículos indefinidos*)

In English, indefinite articles are *a* and *an*. In Spanish, just like with the definite articles, we have one for masculine nouns and one for feminine nouns: *un* and *una*.

Masculine nouns

a phone - un teléfono

a game - un juego

a pen - un bolígrafo

a road - un camino

a notebook - un cuaderno

a book - un libro

a shoe - un zapato

a tree - un árbol

a coffee - un café

a problem - un problema

Feminine nouns

a door - una puerta

a chair - una silla

a kitchen - una cocina

a party - una fiesta

a table - una mesa

a night - una noche

a class - una clase

a picture - una foto

a hand - una mano

an image - una imagen

a person - una persona

When it comes to plurals, in English you would say *some* or *a few*. In Spanish, we say *unos* or *unas*. Examples:

I saw him **a few** days ago - Lo vi hace **unos** días

I brought you **some** apples - Te traje **unas** manzanas

I have **some** terrible mosquito bites - Tengo **unas** picaduras de mosquito terribles

Some unknown men visited her - **Unos** hombres desconocidos la visitaron

Exercises

I want a new phone - Quiero …. teléfono nuevo

Find the door and use it! - ¡Encuentra …. puerta y úsala!

Let's play some games - Juguemos ………. juegos

It was my grandmother's chair - Era …. silla de mi abuela

Give me back the pen - Devuélveme …. bolígrafo

I've never seen such a big kitchen - Nunca vi …. cocina tan grande

We have to go back to the road - Debemos volver …. camino

I was invited to Martina's party - Me invitaron a …. fiesta de Martina

What do you write in the notebook I gave you? - ¿Qué escribes en …. cuaderno que te di?

We need a new table - Necesitamos …. nueva mesa

I bought some new books - Compré ………. libros nuevos

Do you remember the night we met? - ¿Recuerdas …. noche cuando nos conocimos?

I lost a shoe - Perdí …. zapato

I'm going to take an advanced class - Voy a tomar …. clase avanzada

Jump from the tree! - ¡Salta….. árbol!

Where are the pictures from the trip? - ¿Dónde están …. fotos del viaje?

I need a coffee - Necesito …. café

That man is a problem - Ese hombre es …. problema

Chapter 6 – Numbers (*números*)

Cardinal numbers (*números cardinales*)

0 - cero

1 - uno/un/una

2 - dos

3 - tres

4 - cuatro

5 - cinco

6 - seis

7 - siete

8 - ocho

9 - nueve

10 - diez

11 - once

12 - doce

13 - trece

14 - catorce

15 - quince

16 - dieciséis

17 - diecisiete

18 - dieciocho

19 - diecinueve

20 - veinte

21 - veintiuno

22 - veintidós

23 - veintitrés

24 - veinticuatro

25 - veinticinco

26 - veintiséis

27 - veintisiete

28 - veintiocho

29 - veintinueve

30 - treinta

Cardinal numbers don't have a masculine or feminine gender distinction, except for number 1 when it's used as an indefinite article (in English it would be *a* or *an*, as in "I ate **an** apple today") or as a pronoun. There are also the plurals *unos* and *unas*, which means *some* or *around*. Examples:

I am number **one**! - ¡Soy el número **uno**!

Do you want **one** of my toys? - ¿Quieres **uno** de mis juguetes?

Do you want **one** of my apples? - ¿Quieres **una** de mis manzanas?

Do you want **a** toy? - ¿Quieres **un** juguete?

I remember it was **a** sunny afternoon - Recuerdo que era **una** tarde soleada

One would think he was the bad guy - **Uno** pensaría que él era el tipo malo

I have **some** extra kilos - Tengo **unos** kilos de más

I did his homework **about** twenty times - Hice su tarea **unas** veinte veces

After 30, you have to start spelling numbers with more than one word:

31 - treinta y uno (literally *thirty and one*)

32 - treinta y dos

33 - treinta y tres

40 - cuarenta

41 - cuarenta y uno

42 - cuarenta y dos

43 - cuarenta y tres

50 - cincuenta

51 - cincuenta y uno

52 - cincuenta y dos

53 - cincuenta y tres

All the numbers that end in 0 up to 100 are:

10 - diez

20 - veinte

30 - treinta

40 - cuarenta

50 - cincuenta

60 - sesenta

70 - setenta

80 - ochenta

90 - noventa

100 - cien

After 100, same rules apply, you just have to call 100 *ciento* instead of *cien*:

101 - ciento uno

115 - ciento quince

122 - ciento veintidós

159 - ciento cincuenta y nueve

These are the hundreds:

100 - cien

200 - doscientos

300 - trescientos

400 - cuatrocientos

500 - quinientos

600 - seiscientos

700 - setecientos

800 - ochocientos

900 - novecientos

When you have thousands, you just write separately the number of thousands and the word for *thousand* (*mil*):

1.000 - mil

2.000 - dos mil

3.000 - tres mil

5.000 - cinco mil

15.000 - quince mil

99.000 - noventa y nueve mil

100.000 - cien mil

354.000 - trescientos cincuenta y cuatro mil

You can use the plural of thousand (*miles*), when you're talking about an unspecified amount. You can do the same with *cientos* (*hundreds*) and *millones* (millions).

I have **thousands** of options - Tengo **miles** de opciones

Thousands of students registered - Se inscribieron **miles** de alumnos

In the capital they are **millions**; we are **hundreds** of **thousands** - En la capital son **millones**; nosotros somos **cientos** de **miles**

It's incorrect to say *cientas*, even when we're talking about something feminine:

I have **hundreds** of questions - Tengo **cientos** de preguntas

Hundreds of women participated - Participaron **cientos** de mujeres

Note that, in Spanish, the thousands are marked with a dot (.), not with a comma as in English. Decimals, instead, are marked with a comma. Just like in English, we do not use the dot in some numbers, such as years.

English

1,500

200,000

1.5

2.75

year 1900

Spanish

1.500 (mil quinientos)

200.000 (doscientos mil)

1,5 (uno coma cinco)

2,75 (dos coma setenta y cinco)

año 1900 (mil novecientos)

The word for *million* is *millón*, but don't forget you have to say it in plural when you have more than one:

1.000.000 - un millón

2.000.000 - dos millones

10.000.000 - diez millones

Note that, while in English a billion is a thousand millions, in Spanish we just call a thousand millions *mil millones*. A Spanish *billón* means a million millions.

Exercises

1.523 - ……………………………

…………… - doscientos sesenta y seis mil seiscientos sesenta y seis

999.999 - ……………………………………………………………

……………. - dieciséis mil doscientos

15.500 - ………………………

……………. - diez mil uno

Ordinal numbers (*números ordinales*)

When you write ordinal numbers with numbers, you generally have to put next to it a superscript *o* or *a*, depending on its gender. There is a special rule for masculine ordinal numbers 1 and 3: they can lose the last letter (*o*) when they come before singular masculine nouns.

1°/1er/1^a - primero/primer/primera

2°/2^a - segundo/segunda

3°/3er/3^a - tercero/tercer/tercera

4°/4^a - cuarto/cuarta

5°/5^a - quinto/quinta

6°/6^a - sexto/sexta

7°/7^a - séptimo/séptima

8°/8^a - octavo/octava

9°/9^a - noveno/novena

10°/10^a - décimo/décima

These are the ordinal numbers after 10°:

11°/11^a - decimoprimero/decimoprimera/undécimo/undécima

12°/12^a - decimosegundo/decimosegunda/duodécimo/duodécima

13°/13^a - decimotercero/decimotercera

14°/14^a - decimocuarto/decimocuarta

15°/15^a - decimoquinto/decimoquinta

16°/16^a - decimosexto/decimosexta

17°/17^a - decimoséptimo/decimoséptima

18°/18^a - decimoctavo/decimoctava

19°/19^a - decimonoveno/decimonovena

20°/20^a - vigésimo/vigésima

21°/21^a - vigésimo primero/vigésimo primera

22°/22^a - vigésimo segundo/vigésimo segunda

30°/30^a - trigésimo/trigésima

40°/40ª - cuadragésimo/cuadragésima

50°/50ª - quincuagésimo/quincuagésima

60°/60ª - sexagésimo/sexagésima

70°/70ª - septuagésimo/septuagésima

80°/80ª - octogésimo/octogésima

90°/90ª - nonagésimo/nonagésima

100°/100ª - centésimo/centésima

1.000°/1.000ª - milésimo/milésima

1.000.000°/1.000.000ª - millonésimo/millonésima

Fractions (*fracciones*)

When you have a half of something, you say "medio" or "media" depending on whether the object is masculine or feminine.

½ - medio/media

You express other fractions saying "un" plus the ordinal number corresponding to the denominator.

⅓ - un tercio

¼ - un cuarto

⅛ - un octavo

1/10 - un décimo

1/100 - un céntimo

Finally, here's some basic vocabulary related to numbers:

to add - sumar

to subtract - restar

to multiply - multiplicar

to divide - dividir

the sum - la suma

the difference - la diferencia

the product - el producto

the quotient - el cociente

to equal - igualar

<u>Exercises</u>

Juan was the first one to arrive - Juan fue el …………. en llegar

I remember when I bought my first car - Recuerdo cuando compré mi ………. automóvil

The first time I saw him, it was raining - La …………. vez que lo vi, estaba lloviendo

I'm always second! - ¡Siempre soy la ……………..!

I will explain it to him for the tenth time - Se lo explicaré por …………..vez

In the fourth grade, I fell in love - En …………. grado, me enamoré

Chapter 7 – Time (tiempo)

To talk about the time in Spanish, you just have to know the numbers and a few formulas, because it's not very different from English. These are the basic words you'll need:

time - tiempo

hour - hora

minute - minuto

second - segundo

morning - mañana

noon - mediodía

afternoon - tarde

evening - noche

midnight - medianoche

night - noche

sunrise - amanecer

sunset - atardecer

today - hoy

yesterday - ayer

tomorrow - mañana

the day before yesterday - antes de ayer

the day after tomorrow - pasado mañana

now - ahora

never - nunca

always - siempre

late - tarde

early - temprano

on time - a tiempo / en horario

day - día

week - semana

month - mes

year - año

century - siglo

daily - diario

weekly - semanal

monthly - mensual

yearly - anual

Asking and telling the time (*preguntar y decir la hora*)

To ask for the time, we actually ask what "hour" it is:

What time is it? - ¿Qué hora es?

Another difference with English is that in Spanish we don't have two different words for *evening* and *night*:

It's 9 in the evening - Son las nueve de la noche

When you write in Spanish, it's quite normal to use the 24 hour clock instead of adding "pm" or "am" to the 12 hour clock:

The meeting is at 4 p.m. - La reunión es a las 16:00

There are different ways of writing the time:

16:00

16.00

16 h

4 p. m.

But when you talk in Spanish, you don't normally use the 24 hour clock. Instead you add *de la mañana* (*in the morning*), *de la tarde* (*in the afternoon*) or *de la noche* (*in the evening/night*) after the time:

four a.m. - las cuatro de la mañana

four p.m. - las cuatro de la tarde

eight p.m. - las ocho de la noche

To talk about what time it is, we use the plural conjugation of the verb *ser* (*to be*), except for the 1, when we use the singular conjugation:

It's three in the afternoon - **Son** las tres de la tarde

It's eight o'clock - **Son** las ocho en punto

It's 1 in the morning - **Es** la una de la mañana

Here's how to say and write every hour of the day:

00:00 - las doce de la noche / medianoche

01:00 - la una de la mañana

02:00 - las dos de la mañana

03:00 - las tres de la mañana

04:00 - las cuatro de la mañana

05:00 - las cinco de la mañana

06:00 - las seis de la mañana

07:00 - las siete de la mañana

08:00 - las ocho de la mañana

09:00 - las nueve de la mañana

10:00 - las diez de la mañana

11:00 - las once de la mañana

12:00 - las doce del mediodía / el mediodía

13:00 - la una del mediodía / la una de la tarde

14:00 - las dos de la tarde

15:00 - las tres de la tarde

16:00 - las cuatro de la tarde

17:00 - las cinco de la tarde

18:00 - las seis de la tarde

19:00 - siete de la tarde / siete de la noche

20:00 - ocho de la tarde / ocho de la noche

21:00 - nueve de la noche

22:00 - diez de la noche

23:00 - once de la noche

When you have to write a specific time, you can do it with numbers:

16:45

13:30

21:22

When you're talking, just like in English, you can say the full number or sometimes you can take some 'shortcuts':

quarter to - menos cuarto

ten to - menos diez

five to - menos cinco

o'clock - en punto

quarter past - y cuarto

half past - y media

As you see, it's very similar to English. Examples:

14:45 - las tres menos cuarto

13:30 - la una y media

20:15 - las ocho y cuarto

17:55 - las seis menos cinco

21:50 - las diez menos diez

Exercises

I have to wake up at six a.m. - Tengo que levantarme a las ………………………

Sunrise will be at a quarter to six - El amanecer será a las seis ……………………..

Yesterday I was feeling bad - ……………… me sentía mal

Today I feel good - ………… me siento bien

Tomorrow at half past eight I have a date - Mañana a las ………... y media tengo una cita

When will we see each other? - ¿..................... nos veremos?

Days of the week and months (*días de la semana y meses*)

These are the days of the week. In Spanish, you don't need to capitalize them:

Monday - lunes

Tuesday - martes

Wednesday - miércoles

Thursday - jueves

Friday - viernes

Saturday - sábado

Sunday - domingo

And these are the months, which we also don't capitalize:

January - enero

February - febrero

March - marzo

April - abril

May - mayo

June - junio

July - julio

August - agosto

September - septiembre

October - octubre

November - noviembre

December - diciembre

Seasons and years

In South America, seasons (*estaciones*) are the opposite as in North America and Europe. When it's summer in Spain (from June to September), it's winter in South America, and vice versa. The four seasons are the following:

summer - verano

autumn - otoño

winter - invierno

spring - primavera

When we're talking about years, remember we don't use a dot nor a comma to mark the thousands: we write *1999* instead of *1.999*. Here are some sentences to talk about years:

I was born in the year 1990 - Nací en el año 1990 (mil novecientos noventa)

Monet painted his water lilies in the 1920s - Monet pintó sus nenúfares en los años veinte

Last year I finished college - El año pasado terminé la universidad

Next year I will get married - El año que viene voy a casarme

I will move to Europe next year - Me mudaré a Europa el año próximo

We met some years ago - Nos conocimos hace algunos años

I can't believe it's almost 2020- No puedo creer que ya sea casi el 2020 (dos mil veinte)

Pompeii was destroyed in the year 79 AD - Pompeya fue destruida en el año 79 d. C. (después de Cristo)

Julius Caesar was born in the year 100 BC - Julio César nació en el año 100 a. C. (antes de Cristo)

In a couple of centuries, humans will move out to other planets - En un par de siglos, los humanos se mudarán a otros planetas

I was born in the last century - Nací en el siglo pasado

It's year 2018 - Es el año 2018

Dates (*fechas*)

To write a date, remember in Spanish we don't use the month-day-year system, but the day-month-year system, so 12/06/2018 is the 12th of June, and not the 6th of December. To say a full date, you just need to learn the days of the week, the numbers and the months. While in English the ordinal numbers are frequently used to talk about dates, in Spanish we normally use cardinal numbers. Examples:

Today is Monday, the 7th of January, of year 2018 - Hoy es lunes 7 (siete) de enero del año 2018 (dos mil dieciocho)

My birthday is on December 12th - Mi cumpleaños es el 12 (doce) de diciembre

My father was born on February 24th of 1967 - Mi padre nació el 24 (veinticuatro) de febrero de 1967 (mil novecientos sesenta y siete)

We do use the ordinal number for the first day of the month in Spanish:

Where's the champagne? It's January 1st already! - ¿Dónde está la champaña? ¡Ya es el 1° (primero) de enero!

Age (*edad*)

In Spanish we don't say we *are* a certain amount of years old, but we *have* years. We use the verb *tener*:

How old are you? - ¿Cuántos años tienes?

I am 30 years old - Tengo 30 (treinta) años

I had my first child at 28 - Tuve a mi primer hijo a los 28 (veintiocho) años

You will go out alone when you're at least 17 years old - Saldrás a bailar solo cuando tengas al menos 17 (diecisiete) años

Chapter 8 – Adjectives (*adjetivos*)

While in English they normally go before, in Spanish adjectives are normally put after the noun or pronoun they affect. Another difference is that in Spanish, adjectives must match gender (feminine or masculine), when possible, and quantity (singular or plural).

The **beautiful** car- El automóvil **bello**

The **ugly** house - La casa **fea**

The **fat** cats - Los gatos **gordos**

My **pretty** cousins - Mis primas **bonitas**

In some cases, the adjective can be used before the noun. When you use the adjectives *bueno* (*good*), *malo* (*bad*) and *grande* (*big*), they lose the last letter if you put them before a masculine noun:

A **good** year - Un año **bueno** / Un **buen** año

A **bad** day - Un día **malo** / Un **mal** día

A **big** tree - Un árbol **grande** / Un **gran** árbol

Useful adjectives

good - buen/bueno/buena/buenos/buenas

bad - mal/malo/mala/malos/malas

big - gran/grande/grandes

small - pequeño/pequeña/pequeños/pequeñas

fast - rápido/rápida/rápidos/rápidas

slow - lento/lenta/lentos/lentas

expensive - caro/cara/caros/caras

cheap - barato/barata/baratos/baratas

loud - ruidoso/ruidosa/ruidosos/ruidosas

quiet - silencioso/silenciosa/silenciosos/silenciosas

intelligent - inteligente/inteligentes

stupid - estúpido/estúpida/estúpidos/estúpidas

heavy - pesado/pesada/pesados/pesadas

light - liviano/liviana/livianos/livianas

hard - duro/dura/duros/duras

soft - suave/suaves

easy - fácil/fáciles

difficult - difícil/difíciles

strong - fuerte/fuertes

rich - rico/rica/ricos/ricas

poor - pobre/pobres

young - joven/jóvenes

old - viejo/vieja/viejos/viejas

long - largo/larga/largos/largas

short - corto/corta/cortos/cortas

high - alto/alta/altos/altas

low - bajo/baja/bajos/bajas

mean - malvado/malvada/malvados/malvadas

beautiful - bello/bella/bellos/bellas

ugly - feo/fea/feos/feas

new - nuevo/nueva/nuevos/nuevas

happy - feliz/felices

sad - triste/tristes

safe - seguro/segura/seguros/seguras

dangerous - peligroso/peligrosa/peligrosos/peligrosas

full - lleno/llena/llenos/llenas

empty - vacío/vacía/vacíos/vacías

interesting - interesante/interesantes

boring - aburrido/aburrida/aburridos/aburridas

important - importante/importantes

right - correcto/correcta/correctos/correctas

wrong - incorrecto/incorrecta/incorrectos/incorrectas

clean - limpio/limpia/limpios/limpias

dirty - sucio/sucia/sucios/sucias

Exercises

Practice matching gender and number using any adjective you want from the list.

Mi hermana ………………… es la más ………………… de la casa

Me compró un regalo …………………………..

Tus ojos son muy ………………

La comida callejera es …………………………...

Mi auto no es muy ……………………

Quiero ir a un lugar …………………..

Este lugar está …………………………..

Yo veo el vaso medio ………………………

A veces sois …………………….

¡Qué hombre ………………!

Usted es muy ………………………

Intenta tomar decisiones ………………………..

Tu habitación está muy ………………………

Tus hijas pueden ser un poco …………………………

Las señoras son muy ……………………

Tengo un ……………… presentimiento

Es un ……………… momento

Mi bolsa es demasiado ……………………...

Los vecinos son tan …………………………. que no puedo dormir

Los libros son …………………………...

La montaña es ………………………………

¡Cómo podéis ser tan …………………………!

Eres …………………...

El helado es más …………………… de lo que me gusta

La escuela es demasiado ……………….. para mí

Mi abuelo es …………………....

Son personas ……………………...

Creen que son hombres …………………

Tus tortas son las más ………………. del mundo

No quiero ser tu amigo, ¡eres ………………!

Tus padres son muy ………………………

Cuando sea ………………., viajaré por todo el mundo

Tengo ……………………. expectativas

Tienes las uñas muy ………………………

Tengo un pantalón ………………………

La película fue demasiado ……………………

A veces puedes ser realmente ………………………

Somos realmente ……………………………

Soy …………………...

Tengo un …………………….. proyecto

Fueron nuestros días más ………………………

Mis padres están ……………………………

Esta es una zona ……………………………

Chapter 9 – Adverbs (adverbios)

Just as adjectives modify nouns, adverbs modify verbs. They normally answer "que questions": "how?", "how much?", "when?" and "where?". Luckily, adverbs don't have to match number and gender, which means they're *invariable*. This makes them much easier to use. Just as in English, adverbs are normally placed *after* the verb they modify:

You speak **slowly** - Habláis **lentamente**

I like you **a lot** - Me gustas **mucho**

He complains **constantly** - Se queja **constantemente**

Adverbs of place (*adverbios de lugar*)

These adverbs answer *where* something happens. The most common adverbs of place are the following:

in front of - adelante/delante de

on top of - arriba/encima de

behind - atrás/detrás de

there - ahí/allí/allá

here - aquí/acá

near - cerca

far - lejos

where - donde/adonde

<u>Examples</u>

The truth is **in front of** you - La verdad está **delante** de ti

I left the tickets **on top of** the fridge - Dejé las entradas **encima** del refrigerador

He's probably hiding **behind** the door - Probablemente está ocultándose **detrás** de la puerta

I always wanted to travel **there** - Siempre quise viajar **allí**

We're **here** for you - Estamos **acá** para vos

I want to buy a house **near** my workplace - Quiero comprar una casa **cerca** de mi lugar de trabajo

Don't go too **far**! - ¡No vayas muy **lejos**!

It should be **where** I left it - Debería estar **donde** lo dejé

Adverbs of time (*adverbios de tiempo*)

These adverbs answer *when, for how long* or *how often* something happens. We've seen them in Chapter 7. The most common adverbs of time are the following:

before – antes de

after – después de

later - luego

soon - pronto/próximamente

late - tarde

early - temprano

still - todavía/aún

yet - aún

now - ya/ahora

yesterday - ayer

today - hoy

tomorrow - mañana

always - siempre

never - nunca/jamás

last night - anoche

right away - enseguida

while - mientras

<u>Examples</u>

Call me **before** you come - Llámame **antes** de venir

We can meet **after** class - Podemos vernos **después** de clases

See you **later**! - ¡Nos vemos **luego**!

We'll find out **soon** - Lo descubriremos **pronto**

She's always **late** - Ella siempre llega **tarde**

I want to be there **early** - Quiero estar allí **temprano**

I am **still** in love with him - **Todavía** estoy enamorado de él

They haven't arrived **yet** - No han llegado **aún**

I want to know your answer **now** - Quiero saber tu respuesta **ahora**

I saw it **yesterday** - Lo vi **ayer**

Can we do it **today**? - ¿Podemos hacerlo **hoy**?

We're hiking **tomorrow** - **Mañana** nos vamos de excursión

I will **always** remember this journey - **Siempre** recordaré este viaje

I **never** went there - **Nunca** fui allí

We had an amazing party **last night** - Tuvimos una fiesta increíble **anoche**

I'll be there **right away** - Estaré allí **enseguida**

I thought a lot **while** walking - Pensé mucho **mientras** caminaba

Adverbs of quantity (*adverbios de cantidad*)

These adverbs answer to the question *how much*. The most common adverbs of quantity are the following:

very - muy

little - poco

a lot - mucho

pretty - bastante

more - más

less - menos

some - algo

too much - demasiado

almost - casi

only - solo/solamente

so - tan

so much - tanto

everything - todo

nothing - nada

approximately - aproximadamente

<u>Examples</u>

I am **very** tired - Estoy **muy** cansada

I have **little** time - Tengo **poco** tiempo

I love you **a lot** - Te quiero **mucho**

I am **pretty** anxious - Estoy **bastante** ansioso

We want **more** - Queremos **más**

They gave me **less** than last time - Me dieron **menos** que la vez anterior

I have **some** experience - Tengo **algo** de experiencia

We ordered **too much** - Pedimos **demasiado**

We're **almost** there! - ¡Ya **casi** llegamos!

We should take **only** what's necessary - Deberíamos llevar **solamente** lo necesario

We're **so** lazy! - ¡Somos **tan** perezosos!

I have **so much** to give - Tengo **tanto** para dar

I want to see **everything** - Quiero ver **todo**

Nothing could make me sad now - **Nada** podría ponerme triste ahora

We need **approximately** one kilo of flour - Necesitamos **aproximadamente** un kilo de harina

Adverbs of manner (*adverbios de modo*)

The adverbs of manner are normally formed adding the suffix *-mente* to an adjective. In English, the same happens with the suffix *-ly*. As we said in Chapter 1, adverbs that end in *-mente* (*-ly*) keep the accentuation of the original word, as if the *-mente* suffix weren't there, even though they're alway stressed in the second to last syllable.

easy, easily - fácil, fácilmente

responsible, responsively - responsable, responsablemente

careless, carelessly - descuidado, descuidadamente

clear, clearly - claro, claramente

quick, quickly - veloz, velozmente

There are some adverbs of manner that don't end in *-mente*.

well - bien

bad - mal

regular - regular

slowly - despacio

fast - deprisa/aprisa

like that - así

as - como

on purpose - adrede

worse - peor

better - mejor

Examples

He does everything **easily** - Hace todo **fácilmente**

We must solve this **responsively** - Debemos resolver esto **responsablemente**

I'm tired of things done **carelessly** - Estoy cansada de que las cosas se hagan **descuidadamente**

Say it **clearly** - Dilo **claramente**

Come **quickly**! - ¡Ven **velozmente**!

I feel **well** - Me siento **bien**

I feel **bad** - Me siento **mal**

He's always **regular** - Es siempre **regular**

Transport moves quite **slowly** - El transporte va bastante **despacio**

We're too **fast** for them - Vamos demasiado **aprisa** para ellos

I don't like things **like that** - No me gustan las cosas **así**

64

I'm happy **as** a baby - Estoy feliz **como** un bebé

They did it **on purpose** - Lo han hecho **adrede**

It's **worse** than our first option - Es **peor** que nuestra primera opción

I feel much **better** - Me siento mucho **mejor**

Other adverbs (*otros adverbios*)

yes - sí

no - no

also - también

neither/nor - tampoco

right - cierto

truly - ciertamente/verdaderamente

obvious - obvio

surely - seguramente

maybe - quizá/quizás/tal vez

probably - probablemente

possibly - posiblemente

surely - seguramente

Examples

Yes, I want to go! - **Sí**, ¡quiero ir!

No, don't laugh - **No**, no te rías

They **also** want to come - Ellos **también** quieren venir

I didn't come here to clean **nor** to babysit - Ni vine a limpiar ni **tampoco** a cuidar niños

It's **right**! - ¡Es **cierto**!

It's **truly** remarkable - Es **verdaderamente** remarcable

That's **obvious**! - ¡Eso es **obvio**!

She's **surely** joking - **Seguramente** ella está bromeando

Maybe it was all planned - **Quizá** todo fue planeado

Probably it's better like this - **Probablemente** sea mejor así

It will work... **possibly** - Funcionará... **posiblemente**

You're **surely** tired - **Seguramente** estás cansado

Exercises

Complete the following sentences with adverbs from this section:

.... recordaré este paisaje

Traje .... lo que me pediste

Dicen que los mejores paisajes del mundo están ....

Piensa .... de hablar

Pensé que ya estaban aquí, pero .... están viajando

El museo está .... de la municipalidad

Después de la fiesta de anoche, mi cerebro funciona ....

Comprendo ....de tu idioma

Solía comer ....

La verdad está .... la mesa

Voy a encontrarme con ellos ....

Debes mantener a tus amigos .... y a tus enemigos .... más ....

Tu verdadera personalidad está .... de tu máscara

Vayamos ....antes de que anochezca

Tu actitud es ....agotadora

Gracias a nuestros nuevos trabajos, viajamos ....

Tus amigos están .... para ti

Esto ha ido demasiado ....

Las llaves aparecerán .... menos lo esperes

¿Por qué eres .... bueno?

.... fue el mejor día de mi vida

.... pensé que las cosas teminarían así

Juguemos a las cartas .... de cenar

¡Hay .... que me gustaría ver en este viaje!

.... vosotros sereis padres y comprenderéis de qué hablo

La gente aquí .... llega ....

En otros países, en cambio, la gente .... llega ....

.... me fui a dormir temprano

El sol sale muy ....

El momento es ....

Los conozco hace .... tiempo

Podemos resolver esto ....si todos cooperamos

Hay .... por hacer en este país, pero no puedo hacer.................

No dejes para .... lo que puedes hacer.........................

¡..........................voy!

No sé qué hacer .... espero

Me gustaría seguir, pero estoy ....cansado

Quiero ir a .... países como este

Cada vez tengo .... miedo a lo desconocido

Necesito un guía que trabaje.............................

Eres .... charlatán

No hay .... peor que eso

.... pierdo el avión

Estamos a .... siete kilómetros

¿Cómo puedo hacer las cosas....................?

La comida de este lugar hace que me sienta ....

Conduces ...., ¡podríamos tener un accidente!

...........................no somos bienvenidos

La comida de este lugar es ....

Camina ....para no marearte. Si caminas demasiado ....te desmayarás

Quiero vivir en un lugar ....

Todos se saludan .... si fueran amigos

Chapter 10 – The indicative mood (*el modo indicativo*)

Using the same models we used to introduce the regular verbs ending in *-ar*, *-er* and *-ir*, in this chapter we're going to show how to conjugate the major verbal tenses in the indicative mood.

Presente del indicativo

This is the simpler verbal tense, and it's equivalent to the English simple present: *I love, I fear, I live*.

To love (*amar*)

yo am**o**

tú am**as** / vos am**ás** / usted am**a**

él/ella am**a**

nosotros am**amos**

ustedes am**an** / vosotros am**áis**

ellos/ellas am**an**

To fear (*temer*)

yo tem**o**

tú tem**es** / vos tem**és** / usted tem**e**

él/ella tem**e**

nosotros tem**emos**

ustedes tem**en** / vosotros tem**éis**

ellos/ellas tem**en**

<u>To live (*vivir*)</u>

yo viv**o**

tú viv**es** / vos viv**ís** / usted viv**e**

él/ella viv**e**

nosotros viv**imos**

ustedes viv**en** / vosotros viv**ís**

ellos/ellas viv**en**

<u>Exercises</u>

Martín (abandonar) ……………… la escuela

Los abuelos (ofrecer) ……………… un regalo a sus nietos

La película (aburrir) ……………… a los niños

Pretérito perfecto simple

This verbal tense is a past tense equivalent to the English simple past: *I loved, I feared, I lived.*

<u>To love (*amar*)</u>

yo am**é**

tú am**aste** / vos am**aste** / usted am**ó**

él/ella am**ó**

nosotros am**amos**

ustedes am**aron** / vosotros am**asteis**

ellos/ellas am**ron**

<u>To fear (*temer*)</u>

yo tem**í**

tú tem**iste** / vos tem**iste** / usted tem**ió**

él/ella tem**ió**

nosotros tem**imos**

ustedes tem**ieron** / vosotros tem**isteis**

ellos/ellas tem**ieron**

<u>To live (*vivir*)</u>

yo viv**í**

tú viv**iste** / vos viv**iste** / usted viv**ió**

él/ella viv**ió**

nosotros viv**imos**

ustedes viv**ieron** / vosotros viv**isteis**

ellos/ellas viv**ieron**

<u>Exercises</u>

Yo (comprar) ……………….. un auto

Martina y Juana (comer) ………………. toda la pizza

Nosotros (escribir) …………………. un libro

Pretérito perfecto compuesto

This past tense is widely used and it is equivalent to the English present perfect: *I have loved, I have feared, I have lived*. Instead of using the verb *to have*, in Spanish we use a special verb that is only used in this occasion: *haber*. While *haber* is conjugated, the verb remains the same.

<u>To love (*amar*)</u>

yo **he** am**ado**

tú **has** am**ado** / vos **has** am**ado** / usted **ha** am**ado**

él/ella **ha** am**ado**

nosotros **hemos** am**ado**

ustedes han am**ado** / vosotros **habéis** am**ado**

ellos/ellas **han** am**ado**

<u>To fear (*temer*)</u>

yo **he** tem**ido**

tú **has** tem**ido** / vos **has** tem**ido** / usted **ha** tem**ido**

él/ella **ha** tem**ido**

nosotros **hemos** tem**ido**

ustedes **han** tem**ido** / vosotros **habéis** tem**ido**

ellos/ellas **han** tem**ido**

<u>To live (*vivir*)</u>

yo **he** viv**ido**

tú **has** viv**ido** / vos **has** viv**ido** / usted **ha** viv**ido**

él/ella **ha** viv**ido**

nosotros **hemos** viv**ido**

ustedes **han** viv**ido** / vosotros **habéis** viv**ido**

ellos/ellas **han** viv**ido**

<u>Exercises</u>

¿Quién (tomar) ………………………mis cosas?

Sin darnos cuenta (beber), ………………………. toda la botella

Mis padres nos (prohibir) …………………… salir

Pretérito imperfecto

This verbal tense is sometimes confusing to English-speaking people, because it is also equivalent to the English simple past, but it also works as the past continuous: *I was loving, I was fearing, I was living*. It is a bit of both, since it expresses a continuity in a past action.

<u>To love (*amar*)</u>

yo am**aba**

tú am**abas** / vos am**abas** / usted am**aba**

él/ella am**aba**

nosotros am**ábamos**

ustedes am**aban** / vosotros am**abais**

ellos/ellas am**aban**

<u>To fear (*temer*)</u>

yo tem**ía**

tú tem**ías** / vos tem**ías** / usted tem**ía**

él/ella tem**ía**

nosotros tem**íamos**

ustedes tem**ían** / vosotros tem**íais**

ellos/ellas tem**ían**

<u>To live (*vivir*)</u>

yo viv**ía**

tú viv**ías** / vos viv**ías** / usted viv**ía**

él/ella viv**ía**

nosotros viv**íamos**

ustedes viv**ían** / vosotros viv**íais**

ellos/ellas viv**ían**

<u>Exercises</u>

De niña, (amar) ……………… los dibujos animados

Mis abuelos siempre (recorrer) ………………… el parque de la mano

Siempre (recibir) ……………… el mismo regalo en Navidad: ¡medias!

Futuro simple

This verbal tense is equivalent to English simple future: *I will love, I will fear, I will live.*

<u>To love (*amar*)</u>

yo am**aré**

tú am**arás** / vos am**arás** / usted am**ará**

él/ella am**ará**

nosotros am**aremos**

ustedes am**arán** / vosotros am**aréis**

ellos/ellas am**arán**

<u>To fear (*temer*)</u>

yo tem**eré**

tú tem**erás** / vos tem**erás** / usted tem**erá**

él/ella tem**erá**

nosotros tem**eremos**

ustedes tem**erán** / vosotros tem**eréis**

ellos/ellas tem**erán**

<u>To live (*vivir*)</u>

yo viv**iré**

tú viv**irás** / vos viv**irás** / usted viv**irá**

él/ella viv**irá**

nosotros viv**iremos**

ustedes viv**irán** / vosotros viv**iréis**

ellos/ellas viv**irán**

<u>Exercises</u>

Cuando yo sea grande, (trabajar) .... de abogada

Si el niño se acerca más, el perro (morder) .... su mano

Pase lo que pase, tú (partir) .... al amanecer

Estar + gerundio (presente)

This construction of the present conjugation of verb *estar* + the gerund of the verb is very similar to the English present continuous: *I am loving, I am fearing, I am living*. While the English gerund always ends with *-ing*, the Spanish gerund ends in *-ando* or *-endo*.

<u>To love (*amar*)</u>

yo **estoy** am**ando**

tú **estás** am**ando** / vos **estás** am**ando** / usted **está** am**ando**

él/ella **está** am**ando**

nosotros **estamos** am**ando**

ustedes **están** am**ando** / vosotros **estáis** am**ando**

ellos/ellas **están** am**ando**

<u>To fear (*temer*)</u>

yo **estoy** tem**iendo**

tú **estás** tem**iendo** / vos **estás** tem**iendo** / usted **está** tem**iendo**

él/ella **está** tem**iendo**

nosotros **estamos** tem**iendo**

ustedes **están** tem**iendo** / vosotros **estáis** tem**iendo**

ellos/ellas **están** tem**iendo**

<u>To live (*vivir*)</u>

yo **estoy** viv**iendo**

tú **estás** viv**iendo** / vos **estás** viv**iendo** / usted **está** viv**iendo**

él/ella **está** viv**iendo**

nosotros **estamos** viv**iendo**

ustedes **están** viv**iendo** / vosotros **estáis** viv**iendo**

ellos/ellas **están** viv**iendo**

<u>Exercises</u>

Ahora que vivimos en el campo, finalmente (respirar) .... aire puro

Los vecinos (vender) .... su casa

Ella ya tiene todo resuelto, pero yo todavía (decidir) .... qué hacer

Estar + gerundio (pasado)

This construction of the *pretérito imperfecto* conjugation of verb *estar* + the gerund of the verb is very similar to the English past continuous: *I was loving, I was fearing, I was living.*

<u>To love (*amar*)</u>

yo **estaba** am**ando**

tú **estabas** am**ando** / vos **estabas** am**ando** / usted **estaba** am**ando**

él/ella **estaba** am**ando**

nosotros **estaba** am**ando**

ustedes **estaban** am**ando** / vosotros **estabais** am**ando**

ellos/ellas **estaban** am**ando**

<u>To fear (*temer*)</u>

yo **estaba** tem**iendo**

tú **estabas** tem**iendo** / vos **estabas** tem**iendo** / usted **estaba** tem**iendo**

él/ella **estaba** tem**iendo**

nosotros **estábamos** tem**iendo**

ustedes **estaban** tem**iendo** / vosotros **estabais** tem**iendo** ellos/ellas **estaban** tem**iendo**

<u>To live (*vivir*)</u>

yo **estaba** viv**iendo**

tú **estabas** viv**iendo** / vos **estabas** viv**iendo** / usted **estaba** viv**iendo**

él/ella **estaba** viv**iendo**

nosotros **estábamos** viv**iendo**

ustedes **estaban** viv**iendo** / vosotros **estabais** viv**iendo**

ellos/ellas **estaban** viv**iendo**

<u>Exercises</u>

Cuando me llamaste (pensar) ……………………………..en ti

Antes de contratarnos, usted (correr) ………………………. muchos riesgos

Nosotros (definir) …………………………. nuestro futuro

Ir + infinitivo (futuro)

This construction with the conjugated present tense verb *ir* (*to go*) + the infinitive form of the verb is an a ver usual alternative to the simple future.

<u>To love (*amar*)</u>

yo **voy a** am**ar**

tú **vas a** am**ar** / vos **vas a** am**ar** / usted **va a** am**ar**

él/ella **va a** am**ar**

nosotros **vamos a** am**ar**

ustedes **van a** am**ar** / vosotros **vais a** am**ar**

ellos/ellas **van a** am**ar**

<u>To fear (*temer*)</u>

yo **voy a** tem**er**

tú **vas a** tem**er** / vos **vas a** tem**er** / usted **va a** tem**er**

él/ella **va a** tem**er**

nosotros **vamos a** tem**er**

ustedes **van a** tem**er** / vosotros **vais a** tem**er**

ellos/ellas **van a** tem**er**

<u>To live (*vivir*)</u>

yo **voy a** viv**ir**

tú **vas a** viv**ir** / vos **vas a** viv**ir** / usted **va a** viv**ir**

él/ella **va a** viv**ir**

nosotros **vamos a** viv**ir**

ustedes **van a** viv**ir** / vosotros **vais a** viv**ir**

ellos/ellas **van a** viv**ir**

<u>Exercises</u>

Yo siempre (contar) ………………………………… contigo

Tus regalos lo (sorprender)………………………………..

Hasta que no se enfrente a sus miedos, ella (sufrir) …………………………….

Chapter 11 – The subjunctive mood (*el modo subjuntivo*)

Spanish subjunctive is used to talk about desires, doubts, the unknown, the abstract and some emotions. The subjunctive includes many of the same tenses as the indicative, but in this chapter we're only going to learn the present subjunctive tense and a past subjunctive tense, used in conditional sentences (see Chapter 13).

For English speakers, sometimes the subjunctive can be difficult to understand, but with practice you'll get it. To start, try to remember the following situations where you have to use it:

1. In sentences with two subjects: Sentences with one subject in the main clause and one in the noun clause use subjunctive.

2. When sentences are linked with a relative pronoun: Sentences that have parts linked by a relative pronoun (que, quien, como).

3. When sentences have two verbs, and the first one expresses wishes, emotions, impersonal expressions, recommendations, doubt and denial.

<u>Examples</u>

I need you to **do** something for me - Necesito que **hagas** algo por mí

He wants me to **buy** him the new videogame console - Él quiere que le **compre** la nueva consola de videojuegos

---

They expect us to **solve** everything - Ellos esperan que nosotros **resolvamos** todo

I doubt he **can** make it - Dudo que él **pueda** hacerlo

I want us to **go** on a trip - Quiero que nos **vayamos** de viaje

She refuses to believe he **is** guilty - Se niega a creer que él **sea** el culpable

We hope you **are** the architect we need - Esperamos que **seas** el arquitecto que necesitamos

I hate that you **talk** to me like that - Odio que me **hables** así

I'm glad that you **love** each other again - Me alegra que se **amen** nuevamente

It is necessary that someone **fixes** it - Es necesario que alguien lo **arregle**

He recommended that I **exercise** more - Me recomendó que me **ejercite** más

I wish the food **tastes** as good as it looks - Ojalá la comida **sepa** tan bien como se ve

I wish my son **passes** his driving test - Ojalá mi hijo **apruebe** su examen de manejo

Present subjunctive (*presente del subjuntivo*)

<u>To love (*amar*)</u>

que yo am**e**

que tú am**es** / vos am**es** / usted am**e**

que él/ella am**e**

que nosotros am**emos**

que ustedes am**en** / vosotros am**éis**

que ellos/ellas am**en**

<u>To fear (*temer*)</u>

que yo tem**a**

que tú tem**as** / vos tem**as** / usted tem**a**

que él/ella tem**a**

que nosotros tem**amos**

que ustedes tem**an** / vosotros tem**áis**

que ellos/ellas tem**an**

<u>To live (*vivir*)</u>

que yo viv**a**

que tú viv**as** / vos viv**as** / usted viv**a**

que él/ella viv**a**

que nosotros viv**amos**

que ustedes viv**an** / vosotros viv**áis**

que ellos/ellas viv**an**

<u>To be (*ser*)</u>

que yo **sea**

que tú **seas** / vos **seas** / usted **sea**

que él/ella **sea**

que nosotros **seamos**

que ustedes **sean** / vosotros **seáis**

que ellos/ellas **sean**

<u>To be (*estar*)</u>

que yo **esté**

que tú **estés** / vos **estés** / usted **esté**

que él/ella **esté**

que nosotros **estemos**

que ustedes **estén** / vosotros **estéis**

que ellos/ellas **estén**

<u>To have (*tener*)</u>

que yo **tenga**

que tú **tengas** / vos **tengas** / usted **tenga**

que él/ella **tenga**

que nosotros **tengamos**

que ustedes **tengan** / vosotros **tengáis**

que ellos/ellas **tengan**

<u>To say (*decir*)</u>

que yo **diga**

que tú **digas** / vos **digas** / usted **diga**

que él/ella **diga**

que nosotros **digamos**

que ustedes **digan** / vosotros **digáis**

que ellos/ellas **digan**

<u>To go (*ir*)</u>

que yo **vaya**

que tú **vayas** / vos **vayas** / usted **vaya**

que él/ella **vaya**

que nosotros **vayamos**

que ustedes **vayan** / vosotros **vayáis**

que ellos/ellas **vayan**

<u>To do (*hacer*)</u>

que yo **haga**

que tú **hagas** / vos **hagas** / usted **haga**

que él/ella **haga**

que nosotros **hagamos**

que ustedes **hagan** / vosotros **hagáis**

que ellos/ellas **hagan**

<u>Can (*poder*)</u>

que yo **pueda**

que tú **puedas** / vos **puedas** / usted **pueda**

que él/ella **pueda**

que nosotros **podamos**

que ustedes **puedan** / vosotros **podáis**

que ellos/ellas **puedan**

<u>To see (*ver*)</u>

que yo **vea**

que tú **veas** / vos **veas** / usted **vea**

que él/ella **vea**

que nosotros **veamos**

que ustedes **vean** / vosotros **veáis**

que ellos/ellas **vean**

<u>To give (*dar*)</u>

que yo **de**

que tú **des** / vos **des** / usted **dé**

que él/ella **de**

que nosotros **demos**

que ustedes **den** / vosotros **deis**

que ellos/ellas **den**

<u>To want (*querer*)</u>

que yo **quiera**

que tú **quieras** / vos **quieras** / usted **quiera**

que él/ella **quiera**

que nosotros **queramos**

que ustedes **quieran** / vosotros **queráis**

que ellos/ellas **quieran**

Exercises

Complete the following sentences using the subjunctive mood:

El público quiere que (tú, cantar) …………………… una serenata

Estaremos más tranquilos cuando (nosotros, ganar) ……………………… un buen sueldo

No puedes obligarlo a que te (él, amar)…………..

Espero que el perro no (él, romper) ………………… su juguete nuevo

Mis abuelos quieren que (nosotros, vivir) ……………………… con ellos por un tiempo

No importa cuánto (yo, estudiar)………………………….mis padres nunca estarán satisfechos

Mi esposa quiere que nuestra hija (ella, ser) ………………………..médica

Mi mamá se asegura de que siempre (nosotros, estar) .... felices

El día que (yo, ser) .... el jefe, las cosas cambiarán

No logro que Juan (él, estar) .... tranquilo

Quiero una casa que (ella, tener) ....tres habitaciones

Necesito alguien que (él/ella, decir) .... la verdad

Mis primos quieren que (nosotros, ir) .... de visita

Necesito un masajista que (él, hacer) .... milagros

Cuando (vosotros, poder) ....juntémonos a estudiar

Cuando (tú, ver) .... dónde está el problema, podremos solucionarlo

Necesitamos a alguien que nos (él/ella, dar) .... indicaciones

No conocemos a nadie que (él/ella, querer) .... viajar con nosotros

Dile a Jorge que (él, ir) .... a hacer las compras

Past subjunctive (*pretérito imperfecto del subjuntivo*)

As you will see, there are always two forms for this subjunctive tense. You can use either.

To love (*amar*)

que yo am**ara**/am**ase**

que tú am**aras**/am**ases** / vos am**aras**/am**ases** / usted am**ara**/am**ase**

que él/ella am**ara**/am**ase**

que nosotros am**áramos**/am**ásemos**

que ustedes am**aran**/am**asen** / vosotros am**arais**/am**aseis**

que ellos/ellas am**aran**/am**asen**

To fear (*temer*)

que yo tem**iera**/tem**iese**

que tú tem**ieras**/tem**ieses** / vos tem**ieras**/tem**ieses** / usted tem**iera**/tem**iese**

que él/ella tem**iera**/tem**iese**

que nosotros tem**iéramos**/tem**iésemos**

que ustedes tem**ieran**/tem**iesen** / vosotros tem**ierais**/tem**ieseis**

que ellos/ellas tem**ieran**/tem**iesen**

To live (*vivir*)

que yo viv**iera**/viv**iese**

que tú viv**ieras**/viv**ieses** / vos viv**ieras**/viv**ieses** / usted viv**iera**/viv**iese**

que él/ella viv**iera**/viv**iese**

que nosotros viv**iéramos**/viv**iésemos**

que ustedes viv**ieran**/viv**iesen** / vosotros viv**ierais**/viv**ieseis**

que ellos/ellas viv**ieran**/viv**iesen**

To be (*ser*)

que yo **fuera/fuese**

que tú **fueras/fueses** / vos **fueras/fueses** / usted **fuera/fuese**

que él/ella **fuera/fuese**

que nosotros **fuéramos/fuésemos**

que ustedes **fueran/fuesen** / vosotros **fuerais/fueseis**

que ellos/ellas **fueran/fuesen**

To be (*estar*)

que yo **estuviera/estuviese**

que tú **estuvieras/estuvieses** / vos **estuvieras/estuvieses** / usted **estuviera/estuviese**

que él/ella **estuviera/estuviese**

que nosotros **estuviéramos/estuviésemos**

que ustedes **estuvieran/estuviesen** / vosotros **estuvierais/estuvieseis**

que ellos/ellas **estuvieran/estuviesen**

To have (*tener*)

que yo **tuviera/tuviese**

que tú **tuvieras/tuvieses** / vos **tuvieras/tuvieses** / usted **tuviera/tuviese**

que él/ella **tuviera/tuviese**

que nosotros **tuviéramos/tuviésemos**

que ustedes **tuvieran/tuviesen** / vosotros **tuvierais/tuvieseis**

que ellos/ellas **tuvieran/tuviesen**

<u>To say (*decir*)</u>

que yo **dijera/dijese**

que tú **dijeras/dijeses** / vos **dijeras/dijeses** / usted **dijera/dijese**

que él/ella **dijera/dijese**

que nosotros **dijéramos/dijésemos**

que ustedes **dijeran/dijesen** / vosotros **dijerais/dijeseis**

que ellos/ellas **dijeran/dijesen**

<u>To go (*ir*)</u>

que yo **fuera/fuese**

que tú **fueras/fueses** / vos **fueras/fueses** / usted **fuera/fuese**

que él/ella **fuera/fuese**

que nosotros **fuéramos/fuésemos**

que ustedes **fueran/fuesen** / vosotros **fuerais/fueseis**

que ellos/ellas **fueran/fuesen**

<u>To do (*hacer*)</u>

que yo **hiciera/hiciese**

que tú **hicieras/hicieses** / vos **hicieras/hicieses** / usted **hiciera/hiciese**

que él/ella **hiciera/hiciese**

que nosotros **hiciéramos/hiciésemos**

que ustedes **hicieran/hiciesen** / vosotros **hicierais/hicieseis**

que ellos/ellas **hicieran/hiciesen**

<u>Can (*poder*)</u>

que yo **pudiera/pudiese**

que tú **pudieras/pudieses** / vos **pudieras/pudieses** / usted **pudiera/pudiese**

que él/ella **pudiera/pudiese**

que nosotros **pudiéramos/pudiésemos**

que ustedes **pudieran/pudiesen** / vosotros **pudierais/pudieseis**

que ellos/ellas **pudieran/pudiesen**

To see (*ver*)

que yo **viera/viese**

que tú **vieras/vieses** / vos **vieras/vieses** / usted **viera/viese**

que él/ella **viera/viese**

que nosotros **viéramos/viésemos**

que ustedes **vieran/viesen** / vosotros **vierais/viesen**

que ellos/ellas **vieran/viesen**

To give (*dar*)

que yo **diera/diese**

que tú **dieras/dieses** / vos **dieras/dieses** / usted **diera/diese**

que él/ella **diera/diese**

que nosotros **diéramos/diésemos**

que ustedes **dieran/diesen** / vosotros **dierais/dieseis**

que ellos/ellas **dieran/diesen**

To want (*querer*)

que yo **quisiera/quisiese**

que tú **quisieras/quisieses** / vos **quisieras/quisieses** / usted **quisiera/quisiese**

que él/ella **quisiera/quisiese**

que nosotros **quisiéramos/quisiésemos**

que ustedes **quisieran/quisiesen** / vosotros **quisierais/quisieseis**

que ellos/ellas **quisieran/quisiesen**

Exercises

Complete the following sentences using the subjunctive mood:

El público quería que (tú, cantar) ……………………. una serenata

Estaríamos más tranquilos si (nosotros, ganar) ………………………. un buen sueldo

No podías obligarlo a que te (él, amar)…………...

Esperaba que el perro no (él, romper) …………………. su juguete nuevo

Mis abuelos querían que (nosotros, vivir) .………………………. con ellos por un tiempo

No importaba cuánto (yo, estudiar) ....mis padres nunca estarían satisfechos

Mi esposa quería que nuestra hija (ella, ser) ....médica

Mi mamá se aseguraba de que siempre (nosotros, estar) .... felices

Si (yo, ser) .... el jefe, las cosas cambiarían

No lograba que Juan (él, estar) .... tranquilo

Quería una casa que (ella, tener) ....tres habitaciones

Necesitaba a alguien que (él/ella, decir) .... la verdad

Mis primos querían que (nosotros, ir) .... de visita

Necesitaba un masajista que (él, hacer) .... milagros

Cuando (vosotros, poder) ....nos juntaríamos a estudiar

Cuando (tú, ver) .... dónde estaba el problema, podríamos solucionarlo

Necesitábamos a alguien que nos (él/ella, dar) .... indicaciones

No conocíamos a nadie que (él/ella, querer) .... viajar con nosotros

Le dije a Jorge que (él, ir) .... a hacer las compras

Chapter 12 – The imperative mood (*el modo imperativo*)

The Spanish imperative mood is used to give orders. There are no tenses in the imperative mood, but there is an affirmative and a negative form. It is not used with all pronouns, since you cannot give orders to yourself or to people who isn't there.

As you can see, for the *usted*, *nosotros* and *ustedes* forms, the imperative is formed using the forms of the present subjunctive, which we explained in the previous chapter.

Regular verbs

To love (*amar*)

tú ama / vos amá / usted ame

nosotros amemos

ustedes amen / vosotros amad

To fear (*temer*)

tú teme / vos temé / usted tema

nosotros temamos

ustedes teman / vosotros temed

To live (*vivir*)

tú vive / vos viví / usted viva

---

nosotros viv**amos**

ustedes viv**an** / vosotros viv**id**

Irregular verbs

<u>To be (*ser*)</u>

tú **sé** / vos **sé** / usted **sea**

nosotros **seamos**

ustedes **sean** / vosotros **sed**

<u>To be (*estar*)</u>

tú **está** / vos **está** / usted **esté**

que nosotros **estemos**

ustedes **estén** / vosotros **estad**

<u>To have (*tener*)</u>

tú **ten** / vos **tené** / usted **tenga**

nosotros **tengamos**

ustedes **tengan** / vosotros **tened**

<u>To say (*decir*)</u>

tú **di** / vos **decí** / usted **diga**

nosotros **digamos**

ustedes **digan** / vosotros **decid**

<u>To go (*ir*)</u>

tú **ve** / vos **andá** / usted **vaya**

nosotros **vayamos**

ustedes **vayan** / vosotros **id**

<u>To do (*hacer*)</u>

tú **haz** / vos **hacé** / usted **haga**

nosotros **hagamos**

ustedes **hagan** / vosotros **haced**

<u>To give (*dar*)</u>

tú **da** / vos **da** / usted **dé**

nosotros **demos**

ustedes **den** / vosotros **dad**

Imperative + pronouns

It's very common that object pronouns are attached to the imperative verb.

Tell me what you want to do - **Dime** qué quieres hacer

Tell us more about your family - **Cuéntanos** más sobre tu familia

Buy him something to eat - **Cómprale** algo para comer

Sometimes you can even attach two pronouns, an indirect object and a direct object pronoun (always in that order).

Tell it to us - Dínoslo

Bring it to me - Tráemelo

Buy it for you - Cómpratelo

Negative commands

Orders not to do something are formed with the adverb "no" + present subjunctive, which is explained in the previous chapter.

Don't look at me - No me mires

Let's not buy more bread - No compremos más pan

Don't tell me what to do - No me digas qué hacer

Chapter 13 – Conditional (*condicional*)

Just as in English (with *would* and *could*), this tense is used for hypothetical situations and to make polite requests.

I would love to be a millionaire - Me **encantaría** ser millonario

Could I have a glass of water? - ¿**Podría** tomar un vaso de agua?

Could I have your class notes? - ¿Me **prestarías** tus apuntes de la clase?

I would kill for a good slice of pizza - **Mataría** por una buena porción de pizza

To love (*amar*)

yo am**aría**

tú am**arías** / vos am**arías** / usted am**aría**

él/ella am**aría**

nosotros am**arímos**

ustedes am**arían** / vosotros am**aríais**

ellos/ellas am**arían**

To fear (*temer*)

yo tem**ería**

---

tú tem**erías** / vos tem**erías** / usted tem**ería**

él/ella tem**ería**

nosotros tem**eríamos**

ustedes tem**erían** / vosotros tem**eríais**

ellos/ellas tem**erían**

<u>To live (*vivir*)</u>

yo viv**iría**

tú viv**irías** / vos viv**irías** / usted viv**iría**

él/ella viv**iría**

nosotros viv**iríamos**

ustedes viv**irían** / vosotros viv**iríais**

ellos/ellas viv**irían**

<u>To be (*ser*)</u>

yo **sería**

tú **serías** / vos **serías** / usted **sería**

él/ella **sería**

nosotros **seríamos**

ustedes **serían** / vosotros **seríais**

ellos/ellas **serían**

<u>To be (*estar*)</u>

yo **estaría**

tú **estarías** / vos **estarías** / usted **estaría**

él/ella **estaría**

nosotros **estaríamos**

ustedes **estarían** / vosotros **estaríais**

ellos/ellas **estarían**

<u>To have (*tener*)</u>

yo **tendría**

tú **tendrías** / vos **tendrías** / usted **tendría**

él/ella **tendría**

nosotros **tendríamos**

ustedes **tendrían** / vosotros **tendríais**

ellos/ellas **tendrían**

To say (*decir*)

yo **diría**

tú **dirías** / vos **dirías** / usted **diría**

él/ella **diría**

nosotros **diríamos**

ustedes **dirían** / vosotros **diríais**

ellos/ellas **dirían**

To go (*ir*)

yo **iría**

tú **irías** / vos **irías** / usted **iría**

él/ella **iría**

nosotros **iríamos**

ustedes **irían** / vosotros **iríais**

ellos/ellas **irían**

To do (*hacer*)

yo **haría**

tú **harías** / vos **harías** / usted **haría**

él/ella **haría**

nosotros **haríamos**

ustedes **harían** / vosotros **haríais**

ellos/ellas **harían**

Can (*poder*)

yo **podría**

tú **podrías** / vos **podrías** / usted **podría**

él/ella **podría**

nosotros **podríamos**

ustedes **podrían** / vosotros **podríais**

ellos/ellas **podrían**

<u>To see (*ver*)</u>

yo **vería**

tú **verías** / vos **verías** / usted **vería**

él/ella **vería**

nosotros **veríamos**

ustedes **verían** / vosotros **veríais**

ellos/ellas **verían**

<u>To give (*dar*)</u>

yo **daría**

tú **darías** / vos **darías** / usted **daría**

él/ella **daría**

nosotros **daríamos**

ustedes **darían** / vosotros **daríais**

ellos/ellas **darían**

<u>To want (*querer*)</u>

yo **querría**

tú **querrías** / vos **querrías** / usted **querría**

él/ella **querría**

nosotros **querríamos**

ustedes **querrían** / vosotros **querríais**

ellos/ellas **querrían**

Past subjunctive + conditional

Conditional sentences use the past subjunctive, which is explained in Chapter 11, and the conditional tense. Just as in English you use *if* to introduce this kind of sentences, in Spanish we use *si*, which is different from *sí* (*yes*), because it doesn't have a *tilde*.

If I **were** rich, I **would buy** you a mansion - Si yo **fuera** rico, te **compraría** una mansión

If they **had** any brains, they **would stay away** from that scam - Si **tuvieran** cerebro, **se alejarían** de esa estafa

If I **had** the time, I **could start** a new major - Si **tuviera** tiempo, **podría** comenzar una nueva carrera

Exercises

Si (yo, comer) ……………….. bien, (yo, tener) …………………… más energía

Si me (tú, decir) ………………… qué necesitas, (yo, poder) …………………… ayudarte

Si (nosotros, tener) ……………………… tiempo, (nosotros, ir) …………………… al cine esta noche

Si me (usted, respetar) ……………………………………….no me (usted, hablar) ……………………… en ese tono

Si me (tú, amar) …………………………..me (tú, cuidar) ……………………………

Chapter 14 – Preposiciones (*prepositions*)

Prepositions in Spanish are the following: *a, ante, bajo, con, contra, de, desde, en, entre, hacia, hasta, para, por, según, sin, sobre* and *tras*.

A (to)

Preposition *a* can loosely translate as *to*, but it actually has many uses that differ from the English preposition. Examples:

I am going home - Voy **a** casa

You should go to the supermarket - Deberías ir **al** supermercado

We arrived at 3 pm - Llegamos **a** las 3 de la tarde.

How much are the tomatoes? - ¿**A** qué precio están los tomates?

We are around the corner - Estamos **a** la vuelta de la esquina

The magazine is published twice a month - La revista se publica dos veces **al** mes

You have to turn left - Debes girar **a** la izquierda

Will you call your sister? - ¿Llamarás **a** tu hermana?

I gave the book to Pedro - Le di el libro **a** Pedro

I go to work by foot - Voy **al** trabajo **a** pie

Are you going to go? - ¿Vas **a** ir?

Ante

This preposition can translate as *before* or *in front of*. Examples:

The truth was in front of me - La verdad estaba **ante** mí

Before anything, we must resolve this - **Ante** nada, debemos resolver esto

Bajo

Bajo means *under*, as in the following examples:

I'm under your orders - Estoy **bajo** tus órdenes

The cat is hiding under the blanket - El gato está oculto **bajo** la manta

Con

This preposition means *with*:

I love running with my trainers- Amo correr **con** mis zapatillas

Do it with love - Hazlo **con** amor

I hate eating out with my grandfather - Odio salir a comer **con** mi abuelo

Contra

This preposition means *against*:

I'm running against my cousin in the local elections - Estoy compitiendo **contra** mi primo en las elecciones locales

My team is playing against yours - Mi equipo está jugando **contra** el tuyo

The car crashed against the tree - El auto chocó **contra** el árbol

De

De means *from* and *as*, but also has many other uses:

I am from Honduras - Soy **de** Honduras

The car belongs to my brother - El auto es **de** mi hermano

They want us to leave the pub - Quieren que salgamos **del** pub

The sculpture is made of marble - La escultura es **de** mármol

I am dressed as a pirate - Estoy disfrazado **de** pirata

The store is open from 10 a.m. to 3 p.m. - La tienda abre **de** las 10 de la mañana a las 3 de la tarde

A standing ovation - Una ovación **de** pie

Desde

Desde also means *since* or *from*, and sometimes can be used in the same places as *de*:

I do this since I'm 5 years old - Hago esto **desde** los cinco años

Everything looks better from where you're standing - Todo se ve mejor **desde** donde estás parado

En

En means *in*, *at*, *on*, *during* or *into*. Examples:

I'm never at home - Nunca estoy **en** casa

She's travelling on a boat - Está viajando **en** barco

I'd rather do it during the spring - Preferiría hacerlo **en** primavera

I want someone like that in my life - Quiero a alguien así **en** mi vida

It's on the table - Está **en** la mesa

In the countryside, things are simpler - **En** el campo, las cosas son más sencillas

Entre

Entre normally means *between*, as in the following examples:

The show starts between 2 and 3 in the morning - El espectáculo empieza **entre** las 2 y las 3 de la mañana

I'm in between jobs - Estoy **entre** empleos

I'm lost in the crowd - Estoy perdido **entre** la multitud

Hacia

Hacia normally can translate as *to* or *around*:

I was going straight to her house - Estaba yendo derecho **hacia** su casa

He came around 2 p.m. - Vino hacia las 2 de la tarde

Hasta

Hasta can translate as *up to*, *to* or *until*:

I want to swim to the opposite shore - Quiero nadar **hasta** la otra orilla

Let's run until we get tired - Nademos **hasta** que nos cansemos

Para

Depending on the context, *para* can mean *for* or *to:*

I'm going *to* your house - Voy **para** tu casa

I bought a gift for you - Compré un regalo **para** ti

Por

Por can mean *through, near, around, in, by, per, for* and *because of*, depending on the context:

I'm doing it for you - Lo estoy haciendo **por** ti

I'm always slow in the morning - Siempre soy lenta **por** la mañana

I bought it for three dollars - Lo compré **por** 3 dólares

Near my house, there are a lot of shops - **Por** mi casa hay muchas tiendas

We have to pay 100 pesos each - Debemos pagar 100 pesos **por** persona

I visit my parents once a month - Visito a mis padres una vez **por** mes

Según

Según can be translated as *according to*:

We will do it according to the rules - Lo haremos **según** las reglas

According to Roberto, everything is fine - **Según** lo que dijo Roberto, está todo bien

Sin

Sin means the lack of something and sometimes can translate as *without*:

He didn't say a word in the whole day - Estuvo todo el día **sin** decir una palabra

I don't feel like going out - Estoy **sin** ganas de salir

Without job opportunities, it's difficult to take risks - **Sin** oportunidades laborales, es difícil tomar riesgos

Sobre

Sobre means *on, above, on top of* or *about,* as in the following examples:

Clouds are dancing above us - Las nubes bailan **sobre** nosotros

I left the money on the table - Dejé el dinero **sobre** la mesa

We were talking about your future - Estábamos hablando **sobre** tu futuro

Tras

Tras means *after* or *behind*:

After falling asleep for the third time, he was fired - **Tras** quedarse dormido por tercera vez, fue despedido

The father was spying on them behind the door - El padre los espiaba **tras** la puerta

Exercises

All of this time, I was under his charms - Todo este tiempo, estaba ………… sus encantos

I didn't go alone, I went with Inés - No fui sola, fui ……. Inés

Is that a painting by Botero? - ¿Ese cuadro es ….Botero?

The burglar hid under the bed - El ladrón se ocultó ………. la cama

I don't want to do anything during the day - No quiero hacer nada ………. el día

When you come to town, don't forget to visit my family - Cuando vengas …. la ciudad, no olvides visitar …. mi familia

I thought Jeremías was Colombian, but in reality he's from Venezuela - Pensé que Jeremías era colombiano, pero ……. realidad es ……. Venezuela

He stood before the judge and lied - Se paró …… el juez y mintió

I'm here since 8 a.m. - Estoy aquí ………. las 8 de la mañana

What is all of this chocolate for? - ¿……………. qué es todo este chocolate?

Why are you making yelling? - ¿………. qué gritas?

You must take your medicine twice a week - Debes tomar tu medicación dos veces …. la semana

During all this time I was suspecting the wrong person - …………. todo este tiempo sospeché ……. la persona equivocada

He left me speechless - Me dejó ………. palabras

Try to think with the brain, not with the heart - Intenta pensar ……. el cerebro, no ……. el corazón

After thinking a lot about this, I decided to quit - …………. pensarlo mucho, decidí renunciar

I gave all the credit to my team - Di todo el crédito …. mi equipo

I will trade my apple for your orange - Te cambio mi manzana ………. tu naranja

I don't leave my house a lot during the winter - No salgo mucho ……. mi casa …………. el invierno

I have to choose between my two best friends - Debo elegir …………. mis dos mejores amigos

Where is your life going? - ¿…………. dónde va tu vida?

Chapter 15 – Tips for learning a new language (*consejos para aprender un nuevo idioma*)

Are you in the middle of planning your trip? Did you think of everything? First aid kit, papers & documents? Very good, but what about your foreign language skills? Have you ever thought how you'll express yourself? Unfortunately, many travelers neglect this topic and think that with English you can get anywhere. And some also assume that you can communicate well with your hands and feet. The question that you should ask yourself is:

What do I expect from my journey and which goal do I have?

To give you a little motivation, here are 5 advantages of being able to express yourself in the foreign language:

- You get to know the locals much more authentically

- You understand the culture and attitude of people much better

- You can negotiate more effectively

- You do not waste valuable time, because you understand faster

- You feel safer

Just to keep it short: You do not have to learn the foreign language to perfection. But you should be able to communicate well. Here are some tips on how to learn certain basics quickly and effectively.

Are you ready? Okay, then we can start. Depending on how much time you have until the trip, you should use the time well. Which language level you achieve depends entirely on you. Here are some essential recommendations on how to learn a language.

1. Speak from the first day

Unfortunately, many people follow a wrong approach when learning a language. A language is a means of communication and should therefore be lived rather than learned. There is no such thing as an "I am ready now." Therefore, just jump into the cold water and speak already at home from the first day on. That sounds horrible and silly? It does not matter, with time it will get better. It is best to set the goal not to miss a day when you have not used the foreign language in any form. Just try to implement everything you learn directly. So speak, write and think in your foreign language.

2. Immerse yourself in the foreign language at home

This tip actually goes hand in hand with the first recommendation. To learn the foreign language quickly and efficiently, you have to integrate it firmly into your everyday life. It is not enough if you learn a few words from time to time and engage in grammar and pronunciation. This has to be done much more intensively. You have to dive properly into the foreign language. Just bring foreign countries to your home. By so-called "Immersion" you surround yourself almost constantly and everywhere with the learning language.

3. Change the language setting on devices

For example, you could change the menu language of your smartphone or laptop from your native language to your learning language. Since you use your smartphone or your laptop every day, you know where to find something and learn some vocabulary along the way. Of course you can also do the same with your social networks like Facebook and Twitter. But watch out that you are always able to change back the menu language!

4. Use foreign language media

You could, for example, get a foreign language newspaper. If that is not available or too expensive, then there are enough newspapers or news portals where you can read news online. Probably you are already familiar with the news through your native language, then the context is easier if you read the same messages again in the foreign language. Further aids are foreign-language films or series. It's probably best to start with a movie or series that you've already seen in your native language. The slang and common phrases can make it really hard for you. If you realize that you are not understanding it well, try the subtitle in the foreign language. If that does not work, then take the subtitle of your native language and try again. Even music should not be neglected in your foreign-language world. This has the advantage of teaching you a lot about the pronunciation and emphasis. Incidentally, you are getting a lot closer to the culture of the country.

5. Set notes in your apartment

If it does not bother you and others, spread little sticky notes with words in the apartment. Whether this is your toothbrush, the couch or the remote control, just place notes on as many objects and pieces of furniture as possible with the respective name of the object in the foreign language. As a result, you have the vocabulary all day long and memorize it automatically.

6. Learn the most important phrases

Another helpful tip is to think about what words and phrases you'll need before you travel. For example, you could write down how to reserve a hotel room or book a bus ride. Even how to order in the restaurant, ask someone for directions and how to communicate with the doctor or the police. Of course, this book is more than enough and you have all the phrases at one place.

7. Set clear goals

Last but not least, an important piece of advice: Set clear goals. Without goals, you will never get where you want to go. Since you have already booked your flight, you also have a deadline, to which you have reached a goal you have set. To accomplish this, you can now place mini orders. But stay realistic with your goals, especially in relation to your mini goals. If they are too big and not realistically achievable, you may lose your courage and give up. A good tip is also that you record your goals in writing because writing is like having a contract with yourself. It makes your goals more binding and makes you feel more obligated to stick to your schedule. The writing down also has the advantage that you have to formulate your goals more precisely and not forget them so quickly. Do not just try to formulate these goals, but really approach them and implement them.

Here are some examples of how you could define your goals:
- Learn 300 words
- Memorize 5 phrases
- Write an email in the foreign language
- Memorize important questions
- Conduct a talk online via webcam

How can you achieve your goals?
- Set Priorities: Be sure to rank your goals by importance!
- Stay realistic: What is your current life situation?
- Start today: Do not think about tomorrow or yesterday, but start today to reach your goals! The longer you wait, the less likely you are to achieve your goals
- Tell others about it: If others know about your goals, then you will do everything possible to reach them. Otherwise, you would have to admit defeat. This tip could of course make you stress, but will help you to work purposefully!

- Change your habits: You may need to change something in your daily routine to achieve your goals. Do not hesitate and reject bad habits that get in your way!
- Reward yourself: Every time you reach a partial goal, do something good! You know best what that can be!
- Obviously, you do not have to punish yourself, but some people are more likely to do it than to be rewarded for success
- Let the imagination play: Imagine how it is when you reach your goals. What would you be capable of? What would you feel? This will motivate you immensely to work on your goals!

8. Humor

Do not feel sad if it does not work right away. You may be embarrassing yourself in front of a native speaker because you mispronounce a word and make a completely different sense. Nobody will blame you. For most people it means a lot that you try to learn their language. And when they laugh then they do not mean that. But the most important thing is: have fun getting to know a new language! After all, you do not have any pressure, as you do at school.

Mastering the foreign language of your destination country has only advantages. You will learn to understand how people of a particular region think, what fears and worries they have and how they tackle life. You'll become more tolerant and see the world differently and, after your journey, you'll definitely question many ways of thinking of your own culture. Of course, you will also learn a lot of new things abroad, even in foreign languages. But please take the time already and get familiar with the new language before you leave. We promise you, it's worth it!

Conclusion (conclusión)

¡Hola nuevamente!

We really hope you enjoyed our Spanish book!

Now you have the basics to understand this beautiful language: its verbal tenses, its pronouns, its prepositions and much more.

We dare you to challenge yourself and explore Spanish even further, until this book is not longer necessary for you. Read short stories in Spanish, novels, newspapers, websites, watch films and immerse yourself in as many Spanish-speaking countries as you can.

Try every possible food and learn its ingredients and recipe. Ask locals about their slang, their local dishes and customs. Not only you'll end up being absolutely fluent in Spanish, but also you'll make tons of new friends and you'll get to know a lot about the world and different cultures. This will definitely make you feel a richer person.

So, if this is nothing but a starting point, we hope it was useful for you to take your first steps into this amazing, complex, ever-changing language.

¡Buena suerte!

If you enjoyed this book, a review on Amazon would be greatly appreciated.

Thanks for your support!

Part 2: Spanish Short Stories

9 Simple and Captivating Stories for Effective Spanish Learning for Beginners

Introduction

Welcome to our short stories e-book for Spanish students!

People have told stories since language was first created. Both in writing and orally (and also through pictures, music and other means of expression), narrative is present in all periods and cultures of time. Our ability to recount stories, through history, has grown and changed, but this activity's purpose remains the same: to give a message to whoever is listening… or reading.

In this book, we invite you to learn Spanish in one of the most magical ways there are: through reading.

If you just started to learn Spanish and want to enlarge your vocabulary, enrich your comprehension skills and reach a new level, this volume will provide you with precisely what you need. But we do not only want you to increase your vocabulary and get familiar with Spanish syntax, but we also want you to enjoy yourself and to have fun.

If you step into our pages, you will find characters from different Spanish-speaking countries, ranging in all ages.

We hope that these nine short stories inspire you to keep on studying and practicing, and —why not?— travelling.

So come join us on these nine adventures! We will guide you through this beautiful language and its diverse uses and resources while you enjoy reading and stimulating your imagination.

How to use this book

This is a brief section to explain the best way to use this Spanish short stories book for beginners.

You will find nine non-consecutive independent fiction stories. You could choose to read them out of order. Nonetheless, we recommend that you read them in order (especially if your Spanish is not great) because the complexity and difficulty of the vocabulary and grammar increases as you move forward.

In the first pieces, you will find simpler and more universal words, shorter sentences, less subordinate clauses and basic grammar. As you reach the last five stories, you will find vocabulary that is more complex and longer sentences.

Each story is written both in Spanish and English. After each paragraph in Spanish, you will find the literal translation in English. You can choose to read the translated paragraphs in English if you didn't understand something in the original Spanish version, or if you want to make sure you understood everything just fine.

After you finish reading each section, you will find a summary that will synthesize the whole story. After that, there will be a vocabulary section, where you will find the translation to the highlighted words from the text. We encourage you to use the vocabulary section, since it's likely you will find these words along the rest of the book and also while practicing Spanish in real life situations.

After the vocabulary section, there are ten questions to prove to yourself that you understood the story. Five of them are multiple-choice questions and the other five are open-ended for you to complete. These questions are about the plot, the characters and other details from the chapter. Don't rush to answer! Some of the questions are tricky, so you have to read very carefully what we are asking for and think thoroughly about every possible answer to choose your reply accurately.

Finally, you will find the answers section so you can compare your results. No peeking allowed!

Before you start reading, we want to give you a final recommendation that can be very useful, especially if you want to improve your conversational skills: read out loud! This could be very advantageous as you're exercising your pronunciation.

We hope you learn a lot and that you have fun with these nine stories! Enjoy!

Chapter 1 – ¡Me voy! (I'm leaving!)

—¡Me voy! —dice el pequeño Matías.

—I'm leaving! —says little Matías.

Ha **discutido** con sus padres porque no quieren **comprarle** una nueva consola de **videojuegos**.

He has argued with his parents because they don't want to buy him a new videogame console.

Matías entra muy **enfadado** a su **habitación** y **cierra la puerta de un portazo**.

Matías walks very angry into his room and slams the door shut.

—No puedes irte, ¡solo tienes siete años! —dice Matilda, su hermanita, quien estaba recostada en la cama **leyendo** un libro de piratas.

—You can't go, you're only seven years old! —says Matilda, his little sister, who's lying down reading a pirate's book.

—Y tú solo tienes cinco, ¡así que no sabes **nada de nada**! —grita su hermano.

—And you're only five, so you know nothing at all! —her brother shouts.

—¡Oye! Yo no te he hecho nada —dice ella—. **De hecho**, a mí también me gustaría una consola nueva de **videojuegos**…

—Hey! I didn't do anything to you —she says—. In fact, I'd also like a new videogame console…

—Bueno, pues a ti **quizá** te la compren, ¡yo me voy!

—Well, maybe they'll buy it for you, I'm leaving!

Mientras hablan, Matías junta sus juguetes favoritos en una **mochila** roja. Coge la **hucha** donde **guarda** sus **ahorros** y la vacía sobre la cama. Contiene un **billete** de diez euros, uno de cinco euros y tres monedas. **Guarda** el dinero en su **bolsillo**.

While they spoke, Matías gathers his favorite toys in a red backpack. He takes the moneybox where he keeps his savings and empties it on the bed. It contains a ten euros note, a five euros note and three coins. He puts the money into his pocket.

Finalmente, **se abrigó** con un suéter de **lana** y salió.

Finally, he covered himself with a woollen sweater and walked out.

—Espera, ¿de verdad te vas? —pregunta Matilda.

—Wait, are you really leaving? —Matilda asks.

—Pues claro, ¡acostúmbrate a ser **hija única**! ¡No volverás a saber de mí! —contesta Matías, y sale dando otro portazo.

—Well of course, get used to being an only child! You'll never know of me again! —Matías replies, and leaves slamming the door again.

Matilda no sabe qué hacer. Está muy preocupada.

Matilda doesn't know what to do. She is very worried.

Sale de la habitación. Su hermano ya no está.

She walks out of the room. Her brother is no longer there.

—Mamá, papá, ¡creo que Matías **se ha marchado**!

—Mom, Dad, I think Matías has left!

Sus padres no parecen muy preocupados.

Her parents don't look very worried.

—Ah, ¿sí? Ya veremos —dice su madre.

—Oh, is it so? We'll see —says her mother.

—No te preocupes, hija, no irá demasiado lejos —dice su padre.

—Don't worry, girl, he won't go too far —says her father.

Pero Matilda está muy preocupada. Nunca había visto a su hermano tan enfadado y resuelto. Sale al **jardín**.

But Matilda is very worried. She has never seen her brother so angry and determined. She goes out the garden.

En el jardín, solo ve a su perro Max, quien le **ladra** a un **pájaro**. Max es un gran pastor inglés, con **pelaje** blanco y gris. Es muy **torpe** y no es muy inteligente. Matilda lo quiere mucho. Lo usa de **almohada** para dormir la **siesta**.

In the garden, she only sees her dog Max, who is barking to a bird. Max is a big English Shepherd, with white and grey fur. He's very clumsy and not very smart. Matilda loves him a lot. She uses him as a pillow at nap time.

—Max, ¿has visto a Matías? —pregunta Matilda.

—Max, have you seen Matías? —Matilda asks.

El perro se acerca torpemente y la mira confundido.

The dog goes near her clumsily and looks at her confused.

—¿Dónde está Matías? —pregunta Matilda.

—Where is Matías? —asks Matilda.

El perro mira hacia la puerta de entrada de la propiedad, donde se ve la **reja** abierta. Matilda se acerca a la entrada y asoma su pequeña **cabeza** rubia hacia la calle. Viven en un **barrio** muy tranquilo, de casas grandes y árboles altos. Como es domingo, no se ve a mucha gente. Matilda mira hacia un lado y hacia el otro.

The dog looks at the property's entrance door, where the fence is open. Matilda goes near the entrance and sticks her little blonde head out to the street. They live in a very quiet neighbourhood, with big houses and tall trees. Since it's Sunday, not many people can be seen. Matilda looks one way and the other.

—¡Matías! —grita, mirando hacia la izquierda—. ¡Matías! —grita, mirando hacia la derecha.

—Matías! —she screams, looking to her left—. Matías! —she screams, looking to her right.

A su vez, Max ladra.

At the same time, Max barks.

—No está por aquí —dice la niña—. Y si a papá y mamá no les importa dónde está… ¡vamos a tener que ir a buscarlo nosotros!

—He's not around here —says the girl—. And, if Dad and Mom don't care about where he is… we're going to have to go and look for him ourselves!

El perro quiere **detenerla** e intenta **empujarla** de nuevo hacia la casa (es más grande y **fuerte** que ella), pero la niña continúa caminando hacia la calle.

The dog wants to stop her and tries to push her back towards the house (it's bigger and stronger than her), but the girl keeps on walking towards the street.

Con Max detrás de ella, la niña parte a buscar a su hermano.

With Max behind her, the girl goes out to look for her brother.

El primer lugar donde lo busca es en la **tienda** del señor Pedro, **a dos calles** de su casa. Siempre va allí con su hermano a comprar **dulces** y algunos **víveres** que les piden sus padres.

The first place where she goes to look for him is Mr. Pedro's store, two streets away from her house. She always goes there with her brother to buy sweets and some supplies their parents ask them for.

—Señor Perro —dijo la niña (le costaba pronunciar bien su nombre)—, ¿ha visto a mi hermano?

—Mr. Pero —says the girl (she has trouble pronouncing his name right)—, have you seen my brother?

—No, pequeña —dice el señor—. ¿Saben tus padres que estás aquí **sola**?

—No, little girl —says the man—. Do your parents know you're here by yourself?

—¡No estoy sola, señor Perro! Max está conmigo.

—I'm not alone, Mr. Pero! Max is with me.

Max ladra. Ambos **se van**.

Max barks. They both leave.

Después, Matilda va a buscar a su hermano a la puerta de su **escuela**. Como es domingo, no hay nadie en la escuela, pero Matilda piensa que quizá lo encontrará allí. Sin embargo, no está.

Later, Matilda goes to their school gate to look for her brother at. Since it's Sunday, nobody's at school, but Matilda thinks she might find him there. However, he's not there.

Finalmente, Matilda decide ir a buscar a Matías al **parque de juegos**. Sin embargo, se interpone en su camino un enorme perro negro. El terrorífico perro negro le **gruñe** y le ataca.

Finally, Matilda decides to go and look for Matías at the playground. However, an enormous black dog gets on her way. The terrifying black dog growls at her and attacks her.

Por suerte, Max se interpone entre ella y el perro. El perro negro parece muy **malo**, pero Max no deja que se acerque a la niña. Antes de que Matilda pueda reaccionar, los dos perros comienzan a **pelearse**. La niña sale corriendo.

Luckily, Max stands between her and the dog. The dog looks very mean, but Max doesn't let it get close to the girl. Before Matilda can react, the two dogs start fighting. The girl runs away.

Cuando llega al parque de juegos, está **llorando**. El sitio está vacío. No hay rastros de su hermano. Se sienta en una **hamaca**, muy triste. No solo no logró encontrar a su hermano, sino que también **abandonó** a su perro Max en una pelea.

When she arrives to the playground, she's crying. The place is empty. There's no sign of her brother. She sits in a hammock, very sad. Not only she didn't find her brother, but also she's abandoned her dog Max in a fight.

"Soy una **cobarde**", piensa, "Si esto fuera una historia de piratas, ¡**merecería** caminar por el tablón y nadar con los **tiburones**!".

"I'm a coward", she thinks, "If this were a pirate's story, I'd deserve to walk the plank and swim with sharks!".

Para colmo, está comenzando a oscurecer. Matilda tiene **miedo**. No solo por ella, sino porque no sabe dónde puede estar su querido hermano, y no sabe si su perro salió **ileso** de la pelea con el maligno perro negro.

On top of that, it's starting to get dark. Matilda is afraid. Not only for herself, but because she doesn't know where her dear brother might be and she doesn't know if her dog came out unharmed from the fight with the evil black dog.

De pronto, oye una voz que la llama.

Suddenly, she hears a voice calling her.

—¡Matilda! ¡Matilda!

—Matilda! Matilda!

¡Es la voz de su hermano! Matilda se pone de pie sobre la hamaca.

It her brother's voice! Matilda stands on the hammock.

—¡Aquí estoy! —grita.

—Here I am! —she screams.

A lo lejos, ve que se acercan su hermano Matías y su perro Max, seguidos por su mamá y su papá.

From a distance, she sees her brother Matías and her dog Max coming, followed by her mom and dad.

Cuando llegan hasta donde está ella, Matías la **abraza** y Max le lame una **mejilla**.

When they arrive to where she is, Matías hugs her and Max licks one of her cheeks.

—¡Hija! —exclama su padre—. ¿Dónde te habías metido? Salimos a buscarte y nos encontramos con Max, lleno de **rasguños**. Nos trajo hasta aquí.

—Girl! —her father exclaims—. Where had you gone? We went out looking for you and we found Max, all scratched. He brought us here.

—Fuimos a buscar a Matías —explica Matilda.

—We went looking for Matías —Matilda explains.

—Matías nunca se fue de casa—le **contesta** su madre—. Tú no lo recuerdas porque eras muy pequeña, pero cuando Matías tenía tu edad hacía esto **todo el tiempo**. Decía que se iba de la casa, tomaba sus cosas, **fingía** que salía a la calle, y luego se escondía en el **cobertizo**… Solo lo hacía para asustarnos. ¡Y lo logró un par de veces!

—Matías never left the house—her mother replies—. You don't remember because you were little, but when Matías was your age, he did this all the time. He said he was leaving, took his things, pretended to walk out to the street, and then hid in the shed… He only did that to scare us. And he achieved it a few times!

—Es verdad —dice Matías, avergonzado—. Nunca me animé a salir solo de casa en realidad… Pero tú… ¡Pasaste **toda la tarde** sola en la calle! Eres muy **valiente**.

—It's true —Matías says, ashamed—. I never dared to really go out of the house alone… But you… You spent the whole afternoon alone on the streets! You're very brave.

—¡Sola no! —dice Matilda—. ¡Con Max!

—Not alone! —says Matilda—. With Max!

Resumen (Summary)

Matías está enfadado con sus padres y dice que se va de casa. Recoge sus cosas y desaparece. Matilda, su hermana menor, sale a buscarlo por el barrio junto con Max, su perro. Lo busca en una tienda y en la escuela, pero no lo encuentra. De pronto, un gran perro negro aparece y le quiere atacar, pero Max la defiende. Ella sale corriendo sola hacia el parque de juegos, donde se siente sola y triste. Finalmente, llega toda su familia, guiada por Max. ¡Su hermano ni siquiera había salido de la casa!

Summary

Matías is angry with his parents and says he's leaving the house. He picks up his thinks and disappears. Matilda, his younger sister, goes out to look for him together with Max, their dog. She looks for him at a store and at the school, but she doesn't find him. Suddenly, a big black dog appears and wants to attack her, but Max defends her. She runs away alone to the playground, where she feels lonely and sad. Finally, all her family arrives, guided by Max. ¡Her brother hadn't even left the house!

Vocabulario (Vocabulary)

To argue - Discutir

To buy - Comprar

Videogames - Videojuegos

Angry – Enfadado/a

Room - Habitación

Slam the door shut - Cerrar la puerta de un portazo

To read - Leer

Nothing at all - Nada de nada

In fact - De hecho

Maybe - Quizá

Backpack - Mochila

Moneybox - Hucha

Savings - Ahorros

Note - Billete

To save - Guardar

Pocket - Bolsillo

To get cover - Abrigarse

Wool - Lana

Only child - Hijo único/hija única

To leave – Marcharse/Irse

Garden - Jardín

To bark - Ladrar

Bird - Pájaro

Fur - Pelaje

Clumsy - Torpe

Pillow - Almohada

Nap - Siesta

Fence - Reja

Head - Cabeza

Neighborhood - Barrio

To stop - Detener

To push - Empujar

Strong - Fuerte

Store - Tienda

Two blocks away - A dos calles

Sweets - Dulces

Supplies - Víveres

Alone - Solo

To leave - Partir

School - Escuela

Playground - Parque de juegos

To growl - Gruñir

Mean - Malo

To fight - Pelear

To cry - Llorar

Hammock - Hamaca

To abandon - Abandonar

Coward - Cobarde

To deserve - Merecer

Shark - Tiburón

Fear - Miedo

Unharmed - Ileso

Suddenly - De pronto

To hug - Abrazar

Cheek - Mejilla

Scratch - Rasguño

To reply - Contesta

All the time - Todo el tiempo

To pretend - Fingir

Shed - Cobertizo

All afternoon - Toda la tarde

Brave – Valiente

Preguntas (Questions)

1. ¿Por qué Matías está enfadado con sus padres?

    a. Porque quieren comprarle una consola de videojuegos.
    b. Porque quiere ser hijo único.
    c. Porque no quieren comprarle una consola.

2. ¿Qué está haciendo Matilda cuando Matías entra en la habitación?

    a. Leer un libro de historietas.
    b. Leer un libro sobre piratas.
    c. Leer libros.

3. ¿Qué se lleva Matías consigo?

4. ¿Dónde busca Matilda a su hermano antes de salir de casa?

    a. En la escuela, el parque y la tienda.
    b. En el jardín.
    c. En el cobertizo.

5. ¿Con quién sale Matilda?

6. ¿Por qué Matilda le dice "Perro" al dueño de la tienda?

7. ¿Por qué no hay nadie en la escuela?

    a. Todos están buscando a Matías.
    b. Porque es fin de semana.
    c. Porque son vacaciones.

8. ¿Por qué Matilda escapa sola hacia el parque?

    a. Escapa de una pelea entre Max y otro perro.
    b. Porque un perro negro la mordió.
    c. Porque su hermano está en el parque.

9. ¿Quién guía a la familia hasta donde está Matilda?

10. ¿Dónde estaba había estado Matías todo ese tiempo?

Questions

1. Why is Matías angry with his parents?

    a. Because they want to buy him a videogame console.
    b. Because he wants to be an unique son.
    c. Because they don't want to buy him a console.

2. What is Matilda doing when Matías walks into the room?

a. She is reading a comic room.
b. She is reading a book on pirates.
c. She is reading books.

3. What is Matías taking with himself?

4. Where does Matilda look for his brother before she leaves the house?

a. At the school, the park and the store.
b. In the garden.
c. In the shed.

5. Who does Matilda go out of the house with?

6. Why does Matilda call the owner of the house "Pero"?

7. Why is there no one at school?

a. Everybody's looking for Matías.
b. Because it's a weekend.
c. Because it's a holiday.

8. Why does Matilda run away alone to the playground?

a. She's running away from a fight between Max and another dog.
b. Because a black dog bit her.
c. Because her brother is at the park.

9. Who guides the family to where Matilda is?

10. Where had Matías been the whole time?

Respuestas (Answers)

1. c

2. b

3. Juguetes y dinero.

4. b

5. Su perro Max.

6. Porque le cuesta pronunciar su nombre.

7. b

8. a

9. Max.

10. En el cobertizo.

Answers

1. c

2. b

3. Toys and money.

4. b

5. Her dog Max.

6. Because she has a hard time pronouncing his name.

7. b

8. a

9. Max.

10. In the shed.

Chapter 2 – Una gran historia (A great story)

Tiago entra en la cafetería y se sienta en **una mesita** junto a una ventana.

Tiago walks into the coffeeshop and sits at a table next to a window.

Cuando el **camarero** le pregunta qué quiere, **pide** un **café con leche**, dos **medialunas** y el **periódico**.

When the waiter asks him what he wants, he orders a coffee with milk, two croissants and the newspaper.

—Hace **siglos** que no leo un periódico —dice alguien.

—I haven't read a newspaper in ages —says somebody.

Tiago levanta la vista. Se trata de **un señor mayor** que está sentado frente a él en otra mesa pequeña. El hombre tiene un aspecto muy melancólico y **cansado**.

Tiago rises his eyes. It's an old man who's sitting in front of him in other small table. The man looks very melancholic and tired.

—¿A qué se debe, señor? —**pregunta** Tiago.

—Why is that, sir? —Tiago asks.

—En el lugar donde yo vivo no nos **permiten** leer el periódico. Dicen que nos da ansiedad y **miedo** —explica.

—Where I live, it is not allowed for us to read the newspaper. It is said that it makes us anxious and afraid —he explains.

—En el lugar donde... ¿usted vive?

—Where... you live?

—No te asustes, muchacho —dice el señor, riendo—. No me escapé de un **manicomio**, si es lo que estás pensando. Vivo en un asilo de ancianos **a pocas manzanas de aquí**. Todos los años me dejan salir en esta **fecha**, para celebrar mi **aniversario de bodas**.

—Don't be afraid, boy —the old man says, laughing—. I didn't escape from a mental asylum, if that's what you're thinking. I live in a retirement home a few blocks away from here. Every year they let me go out on this date, so I can celebrate my wedding anniversary.

—Eso es muy romántico, señor. ¿Este lugar tiene alguna relación con esa fecha? —pregunta el joven Tiago.

—That's very romantic, sir. Is this place somehow related to that date? —young Tiago asks.

—¡Claro que sí! —dice el anciano—. En esta misma mesa donde estoy sentado **conocí** a mi esposa hace cincuenta y siete años. Esta cafetería, en esa época, era el lugar **de moda** de la ciudad. Todos **se reunían** aquí. Esa **tarde** el sitio estaba **lleno**... Pero estoy seguro de que no quieres escuchar historias de un **viejo** como yo...

—Of course it is! —says the old man—. In this same table where I'm sitting I met my wife fifty-seven years ago. This coffee shop, around that time, was the most popular place in town. Everybody gathered here. That afternoon the place was full... But I'm sure you don't want to hear stories from an old man like me...

—No, por favor, señor, ¡me encantan las historias! ¡Cuénteme más, por favor! Puedo **sentarme** con usted, si lo desea.

—No, please, sir, I love stories! Tell me more, please! I can sit with you, if you wish so.

Tiago coge sus cosas y se sienta en la mesa del hombre viejo.

Tiago grabs his things and sits at the old man's table.

—Como decía, ese día, la cafetería estaba llena. En **esa época**, trabajaba aquí mi **primo** Héctor, el abuelo de aquel joven camarero que te trae el café...

—As I was saying, that day, the coffee shop was full. Around that time, my cousin Héctor worked here. He was the grandfather of that young waiter who's bringing your coffee...

El camarero llega con su **bandeja** y sirve frente a Tiago el café y las dos medialunas. Deja el periódico **doblado** junto a la **taza**.

The waiter arrives with his tray and serves the coffee and the two croissants in front of Tiago. He leaves the folded newspaper next to the mug.

—Mi primo Héctor sabía que yo estaba **soltero**, claro. Como no había más mesas libres, le preguntó a **una joven señorita** que estaba sentada aquí, en esa silla que ocupas ahora, si le molestaba **compartir** la mesa con alguien más. La muchacha no tuvo más opción que decir que sí… y así nos conocimos. Seis meses después, **estábamos casados**. Tuvimos cuatro hijos, todos tan hermosos como ella. Y ahora, solo me queda su **recuerdo**…

—My cousin Héctor knew I was single, of course. Since there were no more free tables, he asked a young girl that was sitting here, in that chair you're occupying right now, if she minded sharing the table with someone else. The girl had no choice than to say yes… and that's how we met. Six months later, we were married. We had four children, all as beautiful as her. And now, I only have my memories of her...

Tiago **se siente conmovido** por la historia. Siente que se le forman **lágrimas** en los ojos. El viejo continúa:

Tiago feels touched by the story. He feels tears forming in his eyes. The old man continues:

—Murió hace casi diez años, pero sigo viniendo aquí en cada aniversario, como cuando estaba viva. Ya no me queda mucho dinero ni mucha memoria, pero todos los años **me aseguro** de tener lo suficiente para venir a tomar un café en nuestro día.

—She died almost ten years ago, but I keep coming here every anniversary, as we used to do when she was alive. I don't have much money or memory left, but every year I make sure to have enough to come here and have a coffee on our day.

Tiago está llorando. Entonces, el señor se dirige al camarero:

Tiago is crying. Then, the man addresses the waiter:

—**La cuenta, por favor**.

—The check, please.

El señor saca una **cartera** vieja de la que empieza a sacar unas **monedas** viejas.

The old man takes out an old wallet from where he starts pulling out some old coins.

—Por favor, señor, déjeme invitarle al café. Esta historia me ha tocado el corazón, realmente me gustaría invitarle.

—Please, sir, let me pay for your coffee. This story has touched my heart, I'd really like to invite you.

—Bueno, muchacho. **Con gusto** aceptaré su invitación, si no es un problema. Ahora ya **se está haciendo tarde**, y tengo ganas de **acostarme**. Voy a volver al asilo antes de perder **las fuerzas**. ¡Camarero! Este joven muchacho pagará mi cuenta.

—Well, boy. I will gladly accept your invitation, if it's not a problem. Now it's getting late and I'd like to lay down. I'm going to return to the retirement home before I lose my strength. Waiter! This young man will pay for my bill.

El hombre se pone su **sombrero**, coge su **bastón**, da **un apretón de manos** afectuoso a Tiago y se marcha caminando lentamente.

The man puts on his hat, grabs his cane, gives Tiago an affectionate handshake and slowly walks away.

—¿Qué historia se ha inventado hoy? —pregunta el camarero.

—What story has he made up today? —the waiter asks.

—**¿A qué te refieres?** —pregunta Tiago, mientras secándose las lágrimas.

—What do you mean? —Tiago asks, while drying his tears.

—Ese viejo **embaucador** se inventa siempre unas historias fantásticas.

—That old crook always makes up some fantastic stories.

—¿O sea que no conoció aquí a su esposa **fallecida**?

—You mean he didn't meet here his deceased wife?

—¿Qué? Conoció a su esposa en otro pueblo y está viva, probablemente esperándolo enfadada en casa. Aquí está la cuenta, muchacho.

—What? He met his wife in another town and she's alive, probably angry and waiting for him at home. Here's the bill, kid.

La cuenta incluye un café, dos medialunas, dos porciones de **estofado** y una botella de **vino caro**.

The bill includes a coffee, two croissants, two servings of stew and a bottle of expensive wine.

Resumen (Summary)

Tiago conoce en una cafetería a un viejo anciano que le cuenta cómo conoció a su esposa hace muchos años en ese mismo lugar. Tiago se conmueve por la historia y decide pagar la cuenta del hombre viejo. Sin embargo, cuando el señor se va, Tiago se entera de que se trataba de un viejo mentiroso.

Summary

Tiago meets an old man at a coffee shop, who tells him how he met his wife many years ago at that same place. Tiago feels touched by the story and decides to pay for the man's bill. However, when the man leaves, Tiago finds out he was a lying old man.

Vocabulario (Vocabulary)

A small table - Una mesita

Waiter - Camarero

To order - Pedir

Coffee with milk - Café con leche

Croissants - Medialunas

Newspaper - Periódico

Century - Siglo

An old man - Un señor mayor

Tired - Cansado

To ask - Preguntar

To allow - Permitir

Fear - Miedo

Mental institution - Manicomio

A few blocks away from here - A pocas manzanas de aquí

Date - Fecha

Wedding anniversary - Aniversario de bodas

To meet - Conocer

Fashionable - De moda

To gather - Reunirse

Afternoon - Tarde

Full - Lleno

Old - Viejo

To sit down - sentarse

That time - Esa época

Cousin - Primo

Tray - Bandeja

Folded - Doblado

Mug - Taza

Single - Soltero

A young lady - Una joven señorita

To share - Compartir

To be married - Estar casado

A memory - Un recuerdo

To feel touched - Sentirse conmovido

Tears - Lágrimas

To make sure - Asegurarse

The check, please - La cuenta, por favor

Wallet - Cartera

Coins - Monedas

Gladly - Con gusto

It's getting late - Se está haciendo tarde

To lay down - Acostarse

Strength - Fuerzas

Hat - Sombrero

Cane - Bastón

A handshake - Un apretón de manos

What do you mean? - ¿A qué te refieres?

Crook - Embaucador

Deceased - Fallecido

Stew - Estofado

Expensive wine - Vino caro

Preguntas (Questions)

1. ¿Qué pidió Tiago?

    a. Dos medialunas, el periódico y un café con leche.

    b. Medialunas, el periódico, un café, una botella de vino y estofado.

    c. Un café con leche.

2. ¿Dónde dice el señor que vive?

    a. En un manicomio.

    b. En un hogar para ancianos.

    c. En otro pueblo.

3. ¿Está Tiago interesado en la historia del señor?

4. ¿Quién dice el viejo hombre que lo ayudó a conocer a su esposa?

    a. El abuelo del camarero.

    b. Su primo Héctor.

    c. Opciones a y b.

5. ¿Por qué estaba llena la cafetería el día en el que el señor supuestamente conoció a su esposa?

6. ¿Cuántos hijos dice el hombre que tiene?

7. ¿Por qué dice el hombre que salió del asilo para ir a la cafetería?

    a. Para celebrar su aniversario.

    b. Para celebrar el cumpleaños de su esposa fallecida.

    c. Porque ha escapado.

8. ¿Quién pide la cuenta?

    a. El viejo.

    b. Tiago.

    c. Ninguno de los dos.

9. ¿Cómo se entera Tiago de que el hombre era un estafador?

10. ¿Qué había bebido el hombre realmente?

Questions

1. What did Tiago order?

    a. Two croissants, the newspaper and a coffee with milk.

    b. Croissants, the newspaper, a coffee, a bottle of wine and some stew.

    c. A coffee with milk.

2. Where does the man say he lives?

a. At a mental institution.
b. At a retirement home.
c. At another town.

3. Is Tiago interested in the old man's story?

4. Who does the old man say helped him get to know his wife?

a. The waiter's grandfather.
b. His cousin Héctor.
c. Options a y b.

5. Why is the coffee shop full on the day the man supposedly met his wife?

6. How many children does the man say he has?

7. For what reason the man says he left the retirement home to go to the coffee shop?

a. To celebrate his anniversary.
b. To celebrate his deceased wife's birthday.
c. Because he has escaped.

8. Who asks for the check?

a. The old man.
b. Tiago.
c. None of the two.

9. How does Tiago find out the man was a crook?

10. What had the man actually drank?

Respuestas (Answers)

1. a

2. b

3. Sí.

4. c

5. Porque era el lugar de moda en esa época.

6. 4.

7. a

8. a

9. Se lo dice el camarero.

10. Vino caro.

Answers

1. a

2. b

3. Yes.

4. c

5. Because it was a fashionable place at that time.

6. 4.

7. a

8. a

9. The waiter tells him.

10. Expensive wine.

Chapter 3 – Los nombres (The names)

Fran entra a la tienda. Se le ve muy **triste**. Sus **compañeros de trabajo** jamás lo han visto así antes.

Fran walks into the store. He looks very sad. His coworkers have never seen him like that before.

Su mejor amigo de la **tienda de quesos** se llama Facundo, pero todos le dicen Rojo, por su cabello pelirrojo.

His best friend from the store is called Facundo, but everybody calls him Red, because of his red hair.

Al ver entrar a Fran, Rojo le dice:

When he sees Fran walking inside, Red says:

—¡Fran! ¿Qué pasa? Tienes un **aspecto** horrible…

—Fran! What's wrong? You look terrible…

—Es el peor día de mi vida —contesta Fran—. Ven fuera conmigo y verás de qué te hablo.

—It's the worst day of my life —Fran replies—. Come with me outside and you'll see what I'm talking about.

Rojo va con su amigo a **la acera**. Al otro lado de la calle, un pequeño **camión de mudanzas** está **aparcado** en frente de un **edificio**. Una joven muchacha ve cómo los empleados de la empresa de mudanzas **guardan** sus **muebles** en el camión.

Red walks with his friend to the sidewalk. On the other side of the road, a small moving truck is parked in front of a building. A young woman watches how the movers put her furniture on the truck.

—¡No! —exclama Rojo—. ¿Se va?

—No! —Red exclaims—. She's leaving?

—**Eso parece** —dice Fran—. Se va y nunca le dije que estoy enamorado de ella. ¡Ni siquiera sé su nombre!

—It looks like it —Fran says—. She's leaving and I never told her I'm in love with her. I don't even know her name!

En ese momento, la muchacha mira en su dirección y les **saluda con la mano**. Ambos **sonríen** y saludan también, antes de entrar al local de nuevo.

At that moment, the girl looks at them and waves. They both smile and wave back, before going back into the store.

—Sabía que esto iba a pasar en algún momento —dice Fran, mientras se pone su delantal y sus guantes de trabajo—. Me dijo que estaba a punto de terminar sus estudios universitarios. Seguramente se va a empezar una nueva vida en otra ciudad, o quizá va a viajar **durante un tiempo** antes de empezar a trabajar… **De cualquier forma**, no querrá saber nada de un simple vendedor de queso como yo.

—I knew this would happen eventually —Fran says, while putting on his apron and working gloves—. She told me she was about to finish her university studies. She will surely start a new life at some other town, or maybe she'll travel for some time before starting to work… Anyhow, she won't want to know anything from a simple cheesemonger like me.

—Pero amigo, ¡si estás estudiando para ser **abogado**! —dice Rojo, mientras cubre su cabello pelirrojo con una red.

—But, mate, you're studying to be a lawyer! —says Red, while he covers his red hair with a net.

—Sí, pero me faltan dos años más… Con el trabajo, **no es fácil**.

—Yes, but I still have two more years to go… While working, it's not easy.

En ese momento, suena la campanilla de la puerta. Alguien ha entrado al local. Es la muchacha de **enfrente**. Lleva una **camisa** celeste y **pantalones** negros. Lleva el cabello recogido en una coleta.

At that moment, the door bell sounds. Someone has come into the store. It's the girl from across the street. She's wearing a light blue shirt and black trousers. Her hair is pulled up in a ponytail.

Parece algo cansada.

She looks a little bit tired.

—Buenos días —dice Rojo con una gran sonrisa—. Nuestra fanática del queso, ¿qué quiere hoy?

—Good morning —Red says with a big smile—. Our cheese fan, what do you want today?

—¡Hola! —responde la muchacha, sonriendo—. Doscientos **gramos** de roquefort, por favor. Voy a **prepararme algo de comer** antes de terminar de **empaquetar** las cosas de la cocina…

—Hello! —the girl replies, smiling—. Two hundred grams of roquefort, please. I'm going to make myself something to eat before I finish to pack my kitchen stuff...

—Te estás mudando, ¿verdad? —pregunta Fran, sin poder ocultar su **decepción**, mientras Rojo comienza a cortar el queso.

—You're moving out, right? —Fran asks, without hiding his disappointment, while Red starts cutting the cheese.

—Sí —dice la muchacha—. **Es una verdadera pena.** Realmente me encantan los quesos de esta tienda… Pero estaré demasiado lejos como para venir cada vez que se me antoje un poco de gruyere o un brie.

—Yes —the girl says—. It's a true shame. I really love the cheeses from this store… But I'll be too far to come here every time I'm craving for some gruyere or brie.

—Lamento que te marches. ¿Has terminado la universidad?

—I'm sorry you're leaving. Are you done with university?

—¡Sí! Hace tan solo una semana. ¡Y ya he conseguido un trabajo! El mismo día que **me gradué** me llamaron desde Australia y me ofrecieron un empleo para hacer **traducciones** de cuentos infantiles al español.

—Yes! Only a week ago. And I already got a job! The same day I graduated I got a call from Australia and I was offered a job to translate children's books into Spanish.

—¡¿De Australia?! —pregunta Fran, **conmocionado**.

—From Australia?! —Fran asks, shocked.

—Sí, increíble, ¿verdad?

—Yes, it's incredible, isn't it?

En ese momento, Rojo entrega a la muchacha su queso en **un paquete**.

At that moment, Red gives the girl the pack of cheese.

—Son 2 euros —dice.

—It's 2 euros —he says.

La muchacha le da **el dinero justo**.

The girl gives him the exact amount of money.

—Quiero agradecerles que hayan sido tan **buenos** conmigo estos dos años que he vivido enfrente. Espero que nuestros caminos vuelvan a cruzarse…

—I want to thank you for being so nice to me these two years I've lived across the street. I hope our paths will meet again...

La muchacha le da la mano a Rojo y a Fran y **las estrecha**. Con una sonrisa melancólica, **se da media vuelta** y sale de la tienda.

The girl extends her arm to Red and Fran and shakes their hands. With a melancholic smile, she turns around and she leaves the store.

Fran está paralizado.

Fran is paralyzed.

—No puedo creer que se haya ido… ¡se me rompe el corazón!

—I can't believe she's gone… my heart is breaking!

—¡Siempre tan dramático, Fran! —contesta Rojo —. Al menos ve y pídele su **correo electrónico**, si tanto te gusta.

—Always so dramatic, Fran! —Red replies—. At least go and ask her for her email, if you like her so much.

Fran sale corriendo de la tienda tras la muchacha, quien ya había cruzado al otro lado de la calle. Sin mirar, Fran **cruza la calle**. No ve que se acerca una bicicleta verde. El hombre que conduce la bicicleta es Jorge, el viejo verdulero de **la esquina**. No logra **frenar** a tiempo, por lo que **choca** contra Fran, quien cae al suelo.

Fran gets out the store, running after the girl, who's already crossed to the other side of the street Without looking, Fran crosses the street. He doesn't see a green bicycle coming his way. The man who rides the bicycle is Jorge, the old greengrocer of the corner. He can't stop in time, so he crashes with Fran, who falls on the ground.

—¿Estás bien? —Es la muchacha, que ha visto toda la escena y se ha acercado corriendo.

—Are you OK? —It's the girl, who has seen the whole scene and has come running.

—Sí —dice Fran—. Don Jorge, **no se preocupe**, no me ha hecho daño.

—Yes —Fran says—. Mr. Jorge, don't worry, you haven't hurt me.

La muchacha ayuda a Fran a **ponerse en pie**.

The girl helps Fran to stand up.

—Te has **hecho daño** en la frente —dice.

—You hurt your forehead — she says.

La muchacha se da la vuelta y abre una de las **cajas** que están sobre el camión de la mudanza. Saca de la caja una botella de alcohol y un trozo de algodón, con los que limpia la herida de Fran.

The girl turns around and opens one of the boxes that are on the moving tuck. She takes out a bottle of alcohol and a piece of cotton from the box, with which she cleans Fran's wound.

El alcohol le produce una sensación de ardor.

The alcohol produces on him a burning sensation.

—**Perdón** —dice ella.

—I'm sorry —she says.

—No hay problema… Solo… Solo cruzaba porque…

—It's not a problem… It's just… I was crossing because…

—¿Sí?

—Yes?

—Porque sé que quizá no vuelva a verte. Pero si voy a **soñar** contigo, al menos me gustaría saber tu nombre. Quiero saber el nombre de la muchacha a la que adoré durante dos años y a la que **extrañaré** por algunos años más.

—Because I know I might not see you again. But if I'm going to dream about you, at least I'd like to know your name. I want to know the name of the girl I adored for two years and that I will miss for a few more years.

La muchacha simplemente lo mira, sin decir nada.

The girl simply looks at him, without saying a word.

—Perdón… —dice Fran—. Soy un poco romántico. Mis amigos se ríen cuando digo cosas así.

—I'm sorry… —Fran says—. I'm a bit of a romantic. My friends laugh when I say things like these.

La muchacha ríe.

The girl laughs.

—No, no. Está bien. Si tengo que **ser sincera**, siempre me has resultado atractivo. ¿Por qué piensas que vengo a comprar queso todos los días desde hace dos años?

—No, no. It's fine. If I have to be honest, I've always found you attractive. Why do you think I come and buy cheese every day since two years ago?

—¿Qué? —exclama Fran—. ¿Y por qué nunca dijiste nada?

—What? —Fran exclaims—. And why did you never say anything?

—¿Y por qué *tú* nunca dijiste nada?

—And why did *you* never say anything?

—Supongo que los dos somos algo **tímidos**.

—I guess we're both a little bit shy.

—Quizá… —dice la muchacha—. **De todas formas**, hay algo que no entiendo. ¿Por qué crees que no vamos a vernos nunca más?

—Maybe… —the girl says—. Anyway, there's something I don't understand. Why do you think we're never going to see each other again?

—Pues… ¡porque te mudas! ¿No te vas a vivir a Australia?

—Well… because you're moving out! Aren't you going to live in Australia?

—No, ¡claro que no! Voy a trabajar **desde mi casa**, de forma remota. Me mudo a unas diez manzanas de aquí. Cerca… aunque lejos como para venir a comprar queso todos los días. Sobre todo, porque tendré una quesería enorme en la esquina.

—No, of course not! I'm going to work from home, remotely. I'm moving ten blocks away from here. Close… though far enough to come and buy cheese every day. Specially, because I'll have a massive cheese store on the corner.

En el rostro de Fran se dibuja una enorme sonrisa.

An enormous smile appears on Fran's face.

—Entonces ¡no te irás! —exclama mientras **salta de la alegría**—. ¡Podemos salir a tomar algo juntos! ¡Te invitaré a cenar este fin de semana!

—Then, you're not leaving! —he exclaims while jumping out of joy—. We can go out and have a drink together! I'll invite you to have dinner this weekend!

—Espera… Tenemos un problema —dice la muchacha.

—Hold on… We have a problem —says the girl.

—¿Qué? —pregunta el muchacho, preocupado.

—What is it? —the boy asks, worried.

—¡Todavía no sé tu nombre!

—I still don't know your name!

—Soy Fran —dice él.

—I'm Fran —he says.

—Yo soy Elisa —dice ella.

—I'm Elisa —she says.

Resumen (Summary)

Fran está muy triste porque la muchacha de la que ha estado secretamente enamorado durante dos años está a punto de mudarse. Él trabaja enfrente de su casa. Después de que la muchacha entre por última vez en la tienda donde él trabaja, él sale corriendo tras ella para confesarle su amor. Al cruzar la calle, sin embargo, choca con una bicicleta. La muchacha le ayuda. Cuando él confiesa lo que ha sentido todo ese tiempo, ella admite que sus sentimientos son iguales y da a Fran una buena noticia: no se muda muy lejos de allí.

Summary

Fran is very sad because the girl he has secretly been in love with for two years is about to move out. He works in front of her house. After the girl goes into the store where he works for the last time, he runs after her to confess his love. While crossing the street, he gets hit by a bicycle. The girl helps him. When he confesses what he has felt all that time, she admits that her feelings are the same and gives Fran a good piece of news: she's not moving far away from there.

Vocabulario (Vocabulary)

Sad - Triste

Coworkers - Compañeros de trabajo

Cheese store - Tienda de quesos

Appearance - Aspecto

The sidewalk - La acera

Moving truck - Camión de mudanzas

Parked - Aparcado

Building - Edificio

Furniture - Muebles

It looks like it - Eso parece

To wave - Saludar con la mano

To smile - Sonreir

For a while - Por un tiempo

Anyhow - De cualquier forma

Lawyer - Abogado

It's not easy - No es fácil

Across the street - Enfrente

Shirt - Camisa

Trousers - Pantalones

Grams - Gramos

To prepare something to eat - Preparar algo de comer

To pack - Empaquetar

Disappointment - Decepción

It's a true shame - Es una verdadera pena

To graduate - Graduarse

Translation - Traducción

Shocked - Conmocionado

A pack - Un paquete

The exact amount of money - El dinero justo

Nice – Bueno/a

To shake hands - Estrechar la mano

To turn around - Darse media vuelta

Email - Correo electrónico

To cross the street - Cruzar la calle

The corner - La esquina

To stop - Frenar

To hit - Chocar

Don't worry - No se preocupe

To stand up - Ponerse en pie

Hurt - Herido

Box - Caja

Sorry - Perdón

To dream - Soñar

To miss - Extrañar

To be honest - Ser sincero

Shy - Tímido

Anyway - De todas formas

From home - Desde mi casa

To jump out of joy - Saltar de la alegría

Preguntas (Questions)

1. ¿Por qué Fran está triste?

    a. Porque le faltan dos años para terminar la carrera.

    b. Porque llegó tarde al trabajo.

    c. Porque la vecina de enfrente se muda.

2. ¿Por qué llaman Rojo a Facundo?

    a. Porque es pelirrojo.

    b. Porque es su color favorito.

    c. Porque tiene el pelo de color.

3. ¿Por qué supone Fran que Elisa se está por mudar?

4. ¿A qué se dedica Fran?

    a. Es abogado.

    b. Se dedica a trabajar.

    c. Estudia y trabaja.

5. ¿Qué ropa lleva Elisa?

6. ¿Qué compra?

7. ¿Cuándo terminó la universidad?

    a. Una semana antes.

    b. Una semana después.

    c. No terminó.

8. ¿En qué consiste el trabajo que consiguió Elisa?

    a. En viajar a Australia.

    b. En escribir cuentos para chicos.

    c. En traducir cuentos para niños.

9. ¿Quién atropella a Fran?

10. ¿Cómo trabajará Elisa para Australia sin irse de su país?

Questions

1. Why is Fran sad?

    a. Because he still has two years to finish college.

    b. Because he's late for work.

    c. Because the neighbour from across the street is moving away.

2. ¿Why do they call Facundo "Red"?

    a. Because he has red hair.

    b. Because it's his favourite colour.

    c. Because he has coloured hair.

3. Why does Fran assume Elisa is about to move away?

4. What does Fran do?

    a. He's a lawyer.

    b. He works.

    c. He studies and works.

5. What is Elisa wearing?

6. What does she buy?

7. When did she finish university?

    a. A week before.

    b. A week later.

    c. She hasn't finished.

8. What is Elisa going to do at her new job?

    a. Travel to Australia.

    b. Write children's books.

    c. Translating children's books.

9. Who runs over Fran?

10. How will Elisa work for Australia without moving away from her country?

Respuestas (Answers)

1. c

2. a

3. Porque hay un camión de mudanzas en la puerta de su casa.

4. c

5. Un pantalón negro y una camisa celeste.

6. Doscientos gramos de roquefort.

7. a

8. c

9. El verdulero de la esquina.

10. De forma remota.

Answers

1. c

2. a

3. Because there's a moving truck in the front of her house.

4. c

5. Black trousers and a light blue shirt.

6. Two hundred grams of roquefort.

7. a

8. c

9. The greengrocer from the corner shop.

10. Remotely.

Chapter 4 – Una pasión de padre e hijo (A father and son's passion)

Ana abrió la **puerta** de su casa después de un largo día de trabajo.

Ana opened her house door after a long day of work.

Su **esposo** la esperaba en la **cocina**. Estaba cocinando.

Her husband was waiting for her at the kitchen. He was cooking.

—¡Hola, mi amor!—, dijo Esteban. Ana lo saludó con una gran **sonrisa** y un **beso**. —¡**Huele delicioso**!

—Hello, my love!—, said Esteban. Ana said hello with a big smile and a kiss. —It smells delicious!

Entonces, Ana se sacó los **zapatos** y fue a **buscar a** sus hijos.

Then, Ana took off her shoes and went to look for her children.

Anita, la más pequeña, leía un **libro de historietas** en la **sala**. Dio un beso a su madre.

Anita, the youngest, was reading a comic book in the living room. She kissed her mother.

Miguel, el mayor, estaba en su **habitación**. Miguel estaba acostado en su cama, mirando el **techo**.

Miguel, the oldest, was in his room. Miguel was lying down, staring at the ceiling.

Ana se dio cuenta de que **algo no iba bien**.

Ana realised that something was wrong.

Las **paredes** de la habitación de Miguel estaban cubiertas de **banderas** del Atlético de Madrid, uno de los dos **equipos de fútbol** más grandes de Madrid.

The walls of the room were covered with banners of the Atlético de Madrid, one of the two biggest football teams from Madrid.

Esteban, el padre de Miguel, era un gran **fanático** del Atlético de Madrid y siempre llevaba a su hijo a ver los **partidos**.

Esteban, Miguel's father, was a great fan of the Atlético de Madrid and always took his son to watch the football games.

Ana dio dos **golpes** en la puerta abierta. Miguel **se sobresaltó**.

Ana knocked on the open door twice. Miguel jumped.

—Mamá, me **has asustado**—, dijo.

—Mom, you scared me—, he said.

—**Perdón**—, dijo Ana. **Se sentó** en la cama. ¿Cuál era el problema de su hijo? Quizá el problema era una niña… o la escuela, pensó Ana. Quizá una **discusión** con un amigo.

—I'm sorry—, said Ana. What was wrong with her son? Maybe it was a girl… or school, Ana thought. Maybe he had had an argument with a friend.

—¿Qué pasa, hijo?—, preguntó Ana, **preocupada**.

—What's wrong, son?—, Ana asked, worried.

—No lo entenderías, mamá… A ti no te gusta el fútbol.

—You wouldn't understand, Mom… You don't like football.

Ana rió. ¡El fútbol! ¿Ese era el problema?

Ana laughed. Football! That was the problem?

—¿Qué ha pasado? ¿Perdió tu **equipo favorito**? ¿Un **jugador** se ha hecho daño?—, preguntó Ana.

—What happened? Did your favourite team lose? Was a player hurt?—, Ana asked.

—No, mamá… ¡ni siquiera es **temporada**!

—No, Mom… the season didn't even start yet!

—¿Entonces qué sucede?

—Then, what is going on?

—No sé cómo decírselo a papá… creo… creo que me gusta el Real Madrid.

—I don't know how to tell Dad… I think… I think I like Real Madrid.

Ana se quedó **atónita**. El Real Madrid era el **equipo contrario** al Atlético de Madrid. Eran los dos grandes **enemigos**.

Ana was stunned. Real Madrid was the team opposite to Atlético de Madrid. They were the two big enemies.

—Desde hace varios meses siento que me gusta más el Real Madrid que el Atlético de Madrid... pero no sé cómo decírselo a papá. Me temo que se le romperá el **corazón**.

—For many months now, I've felt I like Real Madrid better than Atlético de Madrid... but I don't know how to tell Dad. I fear his heart will break.

Ana **tranquilizó** a su hijo: —No creo... Pero solo hay una forma de **averiguarlo**. Debes decírselo.

Ana reassured his son: —I don't think so... But there is only one way to find out. You must tell him.

—No, no puedo hacerlo... no esta noche—, dijo Miguel.

—No, I can't do it... Not tonight—, Miguel said.

La familia comió las pizzas que había cocinado Esteban. Miguel no habló en toda la **velada**. Cuando su padre le preguntó si todo iba bien, **asintió** sin mirarlo a los ojos.

The family ate the pizzas that Esteban cooked. Miguel didn't speak in the whole evening. When his father asked if everything was alright, he nodded without looking at him in the eye.

El día siguiente, en la escuela, sus amigos **se reunieron** en el **recreo** para preguntarle qué le sucedía.

The next day, at school, his friends gathered during the school break to ask him what was going on.

Miguel confesó: —Creo que soy fan del Real Madrid, pero tengo miedo de que mi padre no lo acepte.

Miguel confessed: —I think I'm a Real Madrid sympathiser, but I'm afraid my father will not accept it.

—Mi padre me **mataría** si me cambiara de equipo—, dijo Pedro.

—My dad would kill me if I changed teams—, said Pedro.

—Sí, amigo, mi padre también me mataría—, dijo Manuel.

—Yes, friend, my dad would kill me too—, said Manuel.

—**De cualquier forma,** debes decírselo—, dijo su **mejor amigo**, Joaquín, que era del Atlético de Madrid. —Para mí no es un problema—, añadió.

—Anyhow, you have to tell him—, said his best friend, Joaquin, who was a fan of Atlético de Madrid. —It's not a problem to me—, he added.

Las **palabras** de su mejor amigo le dieron **valor**. Esa noche, cuando llegó a su casa, fue **directo** a la cocina, donde su padre **preparaba la cena**.

His best friend's words gave him courage. That evening, when he arrived home, he went straight to the kitchen, where his father was making dinner.

—Papá, tengo que confesar algo—, dijo. Su padre lo miró muy preocupado. —¿Qué ha pasado, hijo?

—Dad, I have something to confess—, he said. His father looked at him worried: —What happened, son?

—Papá… ¡creo que soy fanático del Real Madrid!

—Dad… I think I'm a Real Madrid fan!

Miguel quería **llorar**. No sabía cuál iba a ser la reacción de su padre. Hasta que finalmente el hombre **rió**…

Miguel wanted to cry. He didn't know what was going to be his father's reaction. Until, finally, the man laughed...

—No me sorprende, hijo, ¡lo llevas en la **sangre**!—, dijo Esteban.

—I'm not surprised, son, it's in your blood!—, said Esteban.

—¡¿Qué?!—, contestó Miguel, —**¿Qué quieres decir?**

—What!?—, replied Miguel, —What do you mean?

—Hijo, creo que nunca te lo dije, mira…—, dijo Esteban mientras buscaba algo en el **armario**.

—Son, I don't think I've ever told you, look…—, said Esteban while he searched for something in the closet.

Volvió con una foto en la que aparecía un niño muy **parecido a** Miguel con una **camiseta** del Atlético de Madrid y un hombre muy parecido a Esteban con una camiseta del Real Madrid.

He came back with a picture where there was a kid very similar to Miguel wearing an Atlético de Madrid shirt and a man very similar to Esteban with a Real Madrid shirt.

—**No entiendo**—, dijo Miguel, —¿Somos nosotros?

—I don't understand—, Miguel said, —Is that us?

Esteban rió.

Esteban laughed.

—No, somos mi padre y yo. Mi padre era fanático del Real Madrid, pero yo siempre simpaticé por el Atlético de Madrid—, contó Esteban.

—No, it's my father and I. My father was a Real Madrid fan, but I always supported Atlético de Madrid—, Esteban told.

—A mi padre le parecía divertido. Antes de los **partidos** entre el Atlético Madrid y el Real Madrid, **apostábamos** una tableta de chocolate al **ganador**—, añadió.

—My father thought it was fun. Before the matches between Atlético de Madrid and Real Madrid we used to bet a chocolate bar to the winner—, he added.

Miguel sonrió. —¿Puedo **guardar** esta foto?—, preguntó a su padre.

Miguel smiles. —May I keep the picture?—, he asked his dad.

—**Claro que sí**—, contestó Esteban.

—Of course—, Esteban replied.

Miguel parecía preocupado.

Miguel seemed worried.

—¿Qué pasa hijo? ¿Te preocupa algo más?—, preguntó Esteban.

—What's wrong, son? Are you worried about something else?, Esteban asked.

—Sí... ¡me preocupan todos los chocolates que vas a tener que comprarme durante la temporada!

—Yes… I'm worried about all the chocolate bars you are going to have to buy during the football season!

Resumen (Summary)

Miguel está preocupado porque ha descubierto que ya no simpatiza por el equipo de fútbol que él y su padre han apoyado siempre, el Atlético de Madrid, sino que ahora es fanático del equipo contrario, el Real Madrid. Se lo cuenta a su madre y a sus amigos de la escuela, y todos le recomiendan que se lo cuente a su padre. Finalmente, decide hacerlo y su padre no reacciona como esperaba: se ríe y le dice que no le sorprende. De hecho, le cuenta a Miguel que lo mismo había sucedido con su propio padre: eran de equipos opuestos.

Summary

Miguel is worried because he has discovered that he no longer likes the football team his father and him have always supported, Atlético de Madrid, but now he's a fan of the opposite team, Real Madrid. He tells his mother and school friends, and they all urge him to tell his father. Finally, he decides to do it and his father doesn't react like he expected: he laughs and he says he is not surprised. In fact, he tells Miguel that the same had occurred with his own father: they were fans of opposite teams.

Vocabulario (Vocabulary)

Door - Puerta

Husband - Esposo

Kitchen - Cocina

Smile - Sonrisa

Kiss - Beso

It smells delicious - Huele delicioso

Shoes - Zapatos

To look for - Buscar a

Comic book - Libro de historietas

Living room - Sala

Room - Habitación

Ceiling - Techo

Something was wrong - Algo no iba bien

Wall - Pared

Banner - Bandera

Football team - Equipo de fútbol

Fan - Fanático

Football game - Partido

Knock - Golpe

To jump - Sobresaltarse

To scare - Asustar

I'm sorry - Perdón

To sit down - Sentarse

Argument - Discusión

Worried - Preocupado

Favourite team - Equipo favorito

Player - Jugador

Season - Temporada

Stunned - Atónito

Opposite team - Equipo contrario

Enemy - Enemigo

To fear - Temer

Heart - Corazón

To reassure - Tranquilizar

To find out - Averiguar

Evening - Velada

To nod - Asentir

To gather - Reunirse

Playtime - Recreo

To kill - Matar

Anyhow - De cualquier forma

Best friend - Mejor amigo

Word - Palabra

Courage - Valor

Straight - Directo

To make dinner - Preparar la cena

To cry - Llorar

To laugh - Reir

Blood - Sangre

What do you mean? - ¿Qué quieres decir?

Closet - Armario

Similar to - Parecido a

Shirt - Camiseta

I don't understand - No entiendo

Match - Partido

To bet - Apostar

Winner - Ganador

Of course - Claro que sí

Preguntas (Questions)

1. ¿Qué estaba cocinando Esteban?

    a. Pasta.
    b. Pizza.
    c. Chocolate.

2. ¿Dónde estaba leyendo Anita cuando Ana llegó a casa?

    a. Un libro de historietas.
    b. La cocina.
    c. La sala.

3. ¿Qué hay en las paredes de la habitación de Miguel?

4. ¿Por qué está preocupado Miguel?

    a. Por una chica.
    b. Porque no sabe cómo contarle algo a su padre.
    c. Por una pelea con un amigo.

5. ¿De qué equipo era fanático el padre de Miguel?

6. ¿De qué equipo era fanático el padre de Esteban?

7. ¿Cómo reacciona el mejor amigo de Miguel cuando le cuenta que es del Real Madrid?

    a. Se enfada.
    b. Se lo dice a su padre.
    c. Lo acepta.

8. ¿Qué objeto le da Esteban a Miguel después hablar?

    a. Una foto.
    b. Una tablet de chocolate.
    c. Una bandera.

9. ¿Quiénes están en la foto?

10. ¿Qué apostaban Esteban y su padre cuando jugaban el Real Madrid y el Atlético de Madrid?

Questions

1. What was Esteban cooking?

    a. Pasta.
    b. Pizza.
    c. Chocolate.

2. Where was Anita reading when Ana arrived home?

    a. A comic book.

    b. The kitchen.

    c. The living room.

3. What was covering Miguel's room walls?

4. Why is Miguel worried?

    a. Because of a girl.

    b. Because he doesn't know how to tell something to his father.

    c. Because of a quarrel with a friend.

5. What football team does Miguel's father support?

6. What football team does Esteban's father support?

7. How does Miguel's best friend react when Miguel tells him he supports Real Madrid?

    a. He gets angry.

    b. He tells Miguel's dad.

    c. He accepts it.

8. What object does Esteban give Miguel after they talk?

    a. A picture.

    b. A chocolate bar.

    c. A banner.

9. Who were in the picture?

10. What did Esteban and his dad bet when Real Madrid and Atlético de Madrid played?

Respuestas (Answers)

1. a

2. c

3. Banderas del Atlético de Madrid.

4. b

5. Atlético de Madrid.

6. Real Madrid.

7. c

8. a

9. Esteban y su padre.

10. Una tableta de chocolate.

Answers

1. a

2. c

3. Atlético de Madrid banners.

4. b

5. Atlético de Madrid.

6. Real Madrid.

7. c

8. a

9. Esteban and his father.

10. A chocolate bar.

Chapter 5 – El huevo podrido (The rotten egg)

Sara, Miguel, Mariano y Dulce eran mejores amigos desde primaria.

Sara, Miguel, Mariano and Dulce were best friends since primary school.

Siempre habían sido **compañeros** de aventuras.

They had always been adventure partners.

Pero ahora que todos tenían vidas **adultas** (trabajos serios, hijos, **deudas**, **electrodomésticos**) rara vez encontraban tiempo para divertirse todos juntos.

But now that they all had adult lives (serious jobs, children, debts, home appliances), they rarely found the time to have fun all together.

Ese sábado, iban a ir a una **cabaña** alejada del centro de la ciudad.

That Saturday, they were going to a cabin removed from the city centre.

Había sido idea de Mariano.

It had been Mariano's idea.

"Es una casita muy **rústica**", le había dicho el dueño **por teléfono** "Ideal para pasar el día".

"It's a very rustic little house", the owner had told him on the phone. "It is ideal to spend the day".

Era **invierno** y había mucha **nieve** en el sur de Chile.

It was winter and there was a lot of snow in the south of Chile.

—¡Es hermosa! —dijo Sara cuando la vio desde el coche.

—It's beautiful! —said Sara when she saw it from the car.

—Un verdadero sueño —añadió Miguel.

—A true dream —added Miguel.

—Se ve muy hogareña —comentó Sara.

—It looks very homey —Sara commented.

—Os lo dije —contestó Mariano.

—I told you so —Mariano replied.

Entraron con sus **provisiones** para pasar el día: **comida**, **bebida**, **juegos de mesa**, revistas, libros y más.

They went in with their supplies to spend the day: food, drinks, board games, magazines, books and more.

—Está completamente **amueblada** —dijo Sara cuando abrió la puerta y pasó al interior.

—It's completely furnished —Sara said when she opened the door and stepped inside.

—Y muy calentita. Parece que los dueños han pasado para encender la **estufa** —dijo Miguel.

—And very warm. It seems the owners have stopped by to turn the stove on —said Miguel.

—Parece que también nos han dejado comida —dijo Dulce, señalando una canasta donde había varios paquetes de pasta, galletas, frascos de mermelada y huevos.

—It seems they have left us some food as well —said Dulce, pointing to a basket with many packages of pasta, biscuits, jam jars and eggs.

—Fue una gran idea venir —dijo Mariano—. Mi idea...

—It was a great idea to come —said Mariano—. My idea...

Los amigos se quitaron los **abrigos** y **se pusieron cómodos** en la cabaña. Pusieron más leña en la estufa, pusieron música, abrieron una botella de vino y se prepararon para relajarse.

The group of friends took off their coats and got comfortable inside the cottage. They put more wood into the stove, put on some music, opened a bottle of wine and got ready to relax.

—¿Queréis que prepare el desayuno? —preguntó Dulce. Miró su reloj—. Más bien será un almuerzo a esta hora.

—Do you want me to prepare lunch? —asked Dulce. She looked at her watch—. It will be more like a brunch at this time.

—Me parece excelente —dijo Miguel. Señaló los huevos de la canasta y añadió—: ¿Qué tal unas tortillas?

—It sound excellent to me —said Miguel. He pointed to the eggs in the basket and added—: How about some omelettes?

Dulce buscó una **sartén** y varios ingredientes más, como **sal** y queso, entre las provisiones que habían llevado.

Dulce looked for a pan and some other ingredients, like salt and cheese, among the supplies they had brought.

Encontró un cuenco para batir los huevos y una batidora.

She found a bowl to beat the eggs and a beater.

Entonces, cuando **partió** el primer huevo, **notó** que algo verdoso asomaba del interior.

Then, when she broke the first egg, she noticed something greenish poking out from the inside.

¡El huevo estaba completamente podrido!

The egg was completely rotten!

En solo un segundo, el **olor** llego a su nariz. ¡Era lo peor que había olido en su vida!

In just a second, the scent reached her nose. It was the worst thing she had smelt in her life!

—TODOS FUERA, ¡DE INMEDIATO! —gritó.

—EVERYBODY OUT, IMMEDIATELY! —she screamed.

Los amigos corrieron al exterior de la cabaña tras ella.

The group of friends run to the exterior of the cabin behind her.

—¿Qué pasa? ¿**se prendió fuego** a algo? —preguntó Sara.

—What happens? Did something set on fire? —Sara asked.

—¿Hay un asesino en serie en la cabaña? —preguntó jocosamente Mariano.

—Is there a serial killer in the cabin? —Mariano asked jokingly.

—No… —dijo Dulce—. ¡Los huevos estaban podridos!

—No… —Dulce said—. The eggs were rotten!

—¡Ay, no! —exclamó Miguel.

—Oh, no! —Miguel exclaimed.

—Vamos, no **será para tanto** —dijo Sara.

—Come on, it can't be that bad —Sara said.

Miguel se rió y le dijo:

Miguel laughed and said to her:

—¿Entonces por qué no entras y nos dices?

—Then why don't you go in and tell us?

Sara aceptó el **desafío** y entró en la cabaña. A los tres segundos, salió cubriéndose la boca con la mano.

Sara accepted the challenge and went into the cabin. Three seconds later, she came out covering her mouth with her hand.

Sus tres amigos se rieron.

Her three friends laughed.

—Bueno, igual vamos a tener que entrar… —dijo Miguel.

—Well, we will still have to go in… —Miguel said.

—Sí. Alguien tiene que sacar el huevo antes de que toda la casa se llene con esa peste.

—Yes. Someone will have to take the egg out before the whole house fills up with that pestilence.

Mariano fue quien **se atrevió** a entrar. Se cubrió la nariz y la boca con el pañuelo que llevaba en el cuello.

Mariano was the one who dared to go in. He covered his nose and mouth with his neckerchief.

A los pocos segundos, salió corriendo con el cuenco que contenía el huevo podrido y lo vació detrás de un árbol.

A few seconds later, he came out running with the bowl that contained the rotten egg and emptied it behind a tree.

—¡Qué horror! —dijo—. Incluso con el pañuelo, ha sido lo más horrible que he olido **en mi vida**. Ahora alguien tiene que entrar a **abrir las ventanas** para que se ventile el lugar. Yo no pienso entrar de nuevo… Puedo llegar a morir.

—How awful! —he said—. Even with the neckerchief on, it was the most horrible thing I smelt in my whole life. Now someone has to go in and open the windows to air the place. I don't plan to go in again… I could die.

La siguiente en animarse a entrar en la casa fue Dulce. Los amigos vieron cómo las ventanas se abrían desde el interior una a una. Cuando salió, aspiró una gran bocanada de aire.

The next one to dare to go in was Dulce. The group of friends saw how the windows were opened from the inside one by one. When she came out she inhaled deeply.

—No me he atrevido a **respirar** en todo el tiempo que he estado dentro —dijo, agitada.

—I didn't dare to breath the whole time I was inside —she said, agitated.

—Será mejor que entre a buscar nuestras cosas, porque puede que estemos aquí fuera **bastante rato** —dijo Miguel.

—It will be better if I go in to get our things, because we might be out here for a while —Miguel said.

Al cabo de unos minutos, tenían sus abrigos, los juegos de mesa y el vino con ellos. Dulce puso **un mantel** en el suelo y se sentaron allí, sobre la nieve. Pasaron un largo rato jugando al dominó. Después, como no podían entrar a **cocinar el almuerzo**, comieron galletas, patatas fritas, nueces, almendras y chocolatinas.

A few minutes later, they had their coats, the board games and the wine with them. Dulce set a tablecloth on the floor and they sat there, on the snow. They spent a long while playing domino. Later, since they couldn't go in to cook lunch, they had biscuits, fries, nuts, almonds and chocolates.

Enfadado por perder al dominó, Mariano arrojó **una bola de nieve** a Miguel. Así comenzó una batalla de bolas de nieve que duró media hora. Armaron dos equipos. Miguel estaba con Dulce y Mariano con Sara. Cuando terminó, se sentaron con una nueva botella de vino a **charlar** y **disfrutar** de la tranquilidad de la tarde.

Angry after losing a domino battle, Mariano threw a snowball to Miguel. That's how a snowball battle that lasted half an hour started. They made two teams. Miguel was with Dulce and Mariano with Sara. When it finished, they sat with a new bottle of wine to chat and enjoy the tranquility of the afternoon.

—Ya no hay olor en la casa —anunció Dulce, que había entrado a la cabaña para usar el baño.

—The house doesn't smell anymore —Dulce announced. She had gone into the cabin to use the toilet.

Los amigos se miraron.

The friends looked at each other.

—Creo que estoy pasando un buen rato aquí afuera de todas formas —dijo Sara—. Hay tanta naturaleza…

—I think I'm having a good time out here anyway —Sara said—. There is so much nature…

—Sí, creo que todos estamos mejor aquí —dijo Miguel—, **¿no es así?**

—Yes, I think we all are better here —Miguel said—, isn't that so?

Los otros **asintieron**. Se quedaron el resto de la tarde en la nieve.

The others nodded. They stayed for the rest of the afternoon on the snow.

Al anochecer, llegó un gran **automóvil** gris. Era el dueño de la casa. Cuando le contaron lo sucedido, soltó una gran carcajada.

At sunset, a big grey car arrived. It was the owner of the house. When they told him what happened, he laughed.

—En esa cesta siempre dejo la comida que dejan los huéspedes. No me di cuenta de que los huevos ya podrían haberse **puesto malos**… Lo lamento mucho.

—I always put into that basket the food that the guests leave behind. I didn't realise the eggs might be bad… I'm very sorry.

—No **se disculpe**, señor. Ha sido lo mejor que nos podía pasar.

—Don't apologise, sir. It's been the best that could happen to us.

Resumen (Summary)

Cuatro amigos van a una cabaña a pasar el día juntos. Sin embargo, nada más entrar, una de ellos quiere preparar una tortilla y ¡el primer huevo que parte está podrido! El huevo huele tan mal que tienen que pasar todo el día fuera de la casa, pero resulta ser lo mejor que les podía pasar.

Summary

Four friends go to a cabin to spend a winter's day together. However, as soon as they go in, one of them wants to prepare an omelette and the egg she breaks happen to be rotten! The egg smells so bad that they have to spend the whole day outside, but it turns out to be the best that could happen to them.

Vocabulario (Vocabulary)

Companions - Compañeros

Grown up - Adulto

Debts - Deudas

Home appliances - Electrodomésticos

Cabin - Cabaña

Rustic - Rústico

On the phone - Por teléfono

Winter - Invierno

Snow - Nieve

Supplies - Provisiones

Food - Comida

Drinks - Bebida

Board games - Juegos de mesa

Furnished - Amueblada

Stove - Estufa

Coats - Abrigos

To get comfortable - Ponerse cómodo/a

Pan - Sartén

Salt - Sal

To break - Partir

To notice - Notar

Smell - Olor

To set something on fire - Prender fuego

To be that bad - Ser para tanto

Challenge - Desafío

To dare - Atreverse

In my life - En mi vida

To open the windows- Abrir las ventanas

To breath - Respirar

A long while - Bastante rato

A tablecloth - Un mantel

To cook lunch - Cocinar el almuerzo

A snowball - Una bola de nieve

To chat - Charlar

To enjoy - Disfrutar

Isn't that so? - ¿No es así?

To nod - Asentir

Car - Automóvil

To go bad - Ponerse malo

Apologise – Disculparse

Preguntas (Questions)

1. ¿De dónde se conocen todos?

    a. Del instituto.
    b. De la universidad.
    c. De primaria.

2. ¿De quién fue la idea de ir ahí?

    a. De Mariano.
    b. Del dueño.
    c. De Dulce.

3. ¿Qué llevaron con ellos?

4. ¿Cómo es el clima?

    a. Nevado.
    b. Lluvioso.
    c. Cálido.

5. ¿Qué encuentran dentro de una cesta?

6. ¿Qué quiere preparar Dulce para el almuerzo?

7. ¿Qué consigue para empezar a cocinar?

    a. Una sartén y sal.
    b. Una sartén, sal, queso y huevos.
    c. Un huevo podrido.

8. ¿Qué hace después de ver que el huevo está podrido?

    a. Incendia algo.
    b. Ve un asesino en serie.
    c. Les dice a todos que salgan.

9. ¿Quién entra en la cabaña después de salir?

10. ¿Se les arruinó el día?

Questions

1. Where did they all know each other from?

    a. Secondary school.
    b. College.
    c. Primary school.

2. Who's idea was it to go there?

a. Mariano's.
b. The owner's.
c. Dulce's.

3. What did they take with them?

4. How is the weather?

a. Snowy.
b. Rainy.
c. Warm.

5. What do they find inside a basket?

6. What does Dulce want to prepare for brunch?

7. What does she get to start cooking?

a. A pan and some salt.
b. A pan, salt, cheese and eggs.
c. A rotten egg.

8. What does she do after she sees the egg is rotten?

a. She sets something on fire.
b. She sees a serial killer.
c. She orders everybody out.

9. Who goes into the cabin after they have to go out?

10. Is their day ruined?

Respuestas (Answers)

1. c

2. a

3. Comida, bebida, juegos de mesa, revistas y libros.

4. a

5. Varios paquetes de pasta, galletas, botes de mermelada y huevos.

6. Tortillas.

7. b

8. c

9. Todos deben entrar.

10. No, es lo mejor que les podría haber pasado.

Answers

1. c

2. a

3. Food, drinks, board games, magazines and books.

4. a

5. Several packs of pasta, biscuits, jam jars and eggs.

6. Omelettes.

7. b

8. c

9. They all have to go in.

10. No, it's the best thing that could have happened to them.

Chapter 6 – Terror en el ático (Horror in the attic)

—Entonces, se abrió la puerta de la casa y salió **una viejita** que le dijo: "¡María está **muerta** desde hace DIEZ AÑOS!" —exclamó Pedro, mientras **encendía** y **apagaba** la linterna bajo su mentón.

—Then, the main door opened and an old lady came out, who told him: "María has been dead for TEN YEARS!" —Pedro exclaimed, while he turned on and off the torch he was holding under his chin.

—¡Eso no **da miedo**! —se **quejó** Rafael.

—That isn't scary! —complained Rafael.

—Claro que sí. ¡Ella había muerto hace diez años! Era un **fantasma**...

—Of course it is. She died ten years ago! She was a ghost…

—Sí, lo he **entendido**. He escuchado esa historia doscientas veces...

—Yes, I got it. I've heard this same story two hundred times…

Pedro y Rafael eran **mejores amigos** de primaria. Ese mismo día, habían terminado quinto de primaria y estaban inaugurando el verano con una noche de **golosinas**, **películas** e **historias de fantasmas**.

Pedro and Rafael were best friends from primary school. That very day they had finished the fifth grade and they were inaugurating the summer with an evening of snacks, movies and horror stories.

En el televisor se veía *Terror en el ático*, una película que ya habían visto muchas veces.

In the television, the film *Horror in the Attic*, which they had seen many times, was playing.

Entre ellos había **cuencos** con patatas fritas, chocolatinas, **bocadillos** de jamón y queso, y bastones de **zanahoria** (los cuales no habían probado).

Between them, there were bowls with crisps, chocolates, ham and cheese sandwiches, and carrot sticks (which none of them has touched).

—Bueno, es tu turno. ¡Ahora *tú* debes contar una historia de terror! —dijo Pedro—. A ver si es tan **sencillo**…

—Well, it's your turn. Now *you* have to tell a horror story! —Pedro—. Let's see if it's so easy...

—Claro que lo haré —contestó Rafael.

—Of course I will —Rafael replied.

Rafael tomó la **linterna** y la colocó debajo de su **mentón**. A continuación, comenzó a narrar con su voz más **siniestra**:

Rafael took the torch and placed it under his chin. Next, he started narrating with his most sinister voice:

—Una noche de verano, dos niños se quedaron solos toda la noche viendo películas de terror y comiendo **golosinas**, hasta que de pronto... Espera, ¿qué fue eso? —preguntó, **asustado**, mirando hacia el techo—. Escuché algo en el piso de arriba.

—On a summer night, two kids stayed alone all night watching horror films and eating sweets, until suddenly… Wait, what was that? —he asked, scared, looking up to the ceiling—. I heard something coming from upstairs.

—¿Qué? No hay **piso** de arriba, solo está el ático... Vamos, Rafael, quieres asustarme.

—What? There is no upstairs, just the attic… Come on, Rafael, you want to scare me.

—No, no, ¡lo juro! Esto no es parte de la historia. ¡He oído algo en el ático! Como unos pasos…

—No, no, I swear! This is not part of the story. I heard something in the attic! Like some steps...

—Me estás mintiendo...

—You're lying to me...

De pronto, se oyó **un golpe** y pasos en el piso superior. **Ambos** amigos se quedaron paralizados. Después de unos segundos, Rafael **se atrevió** a hablar:

Suddenly, there was a bang and steps coming from the upper floor. Both friends froze. After a few seconds, Rafael dared to talk:

—Tranquilo, amigo. Tiene que ser mi **gata**, Petunia. Le encanta el ático.

—Easy, my friend. It has to be my cat, Petunia. She loves the attic.

—No quiero asustarte, Pedro —dijo Rafael—, pero Petunia está **ahí mismo**.

—I don't want to scare you, Pedro —said Rafael—, but Petunia is right there.

La gata negra bebía **agua** de su pequeño cuenco.

The black cat was drinking water from her little bowl.

En ese momento, un fuerte **grito** salió del televisor. Los **protagonistas** de la película habían subido al ático, donde un **asesino** los esperaba. Pedro apagó el televisor y encendió las luces de la **sala**.

At that moment, a loud scream came out of the TV. The main characters of the movie had gone up to the attic, where a killer waited for them. Pedro turned the TV off and lit the living room lights.

—¿A qué hora vuelve tu madre? —preguntó Rafael.

—What time does your mother return home? —asked Rafael.

—¡Se fue hace solo media hora! —dijo Pedro—. No creo que la veamos en un buen rato.

—She left only half an hour ago! —dijo Pedro—. No creo que la veamos en un buen rato.

—¿Deberíamos llamar a **la policía**?

—Should we call the police?

—No sabemos si es una persona. Quizá es una rata, o un **pájaro**... No sé, quizá eran sonidos de la película y lo estábamos imaginando…

—We don't know if it's a person. It might be a rat, or a bird… I don't know, maybe it was sounds from the movie and we were imagining it...

En ese instante, se escucharon dos golpes y un grito muy agudo y lejano. Pedro se asustó tanto que, sin querer, pisó el plato con los bastones de zanahoria.

At that moment, two bangs and a high and distant scream were heard. Pedro got so scared that, accidentally, stepped on the carrot sticks bowl.

—¡Maldición! —exclamó.

—Damn! —He said.

—¿Qué fue ese ruido? Parecía **el llanto** de un bebé... —dijo Rafael.

—What was that noise? It seemed like the crying of a baby... —said Rafael.

Rafael **se acercó** al pasillo.

Rafael moved towards the hallway.

—¡¿A dónde vas?! —exclamó Pedro, siguiendo a su amigo—. No me digas que quieres subir…

—Where are you going?! —exclaimed Pedro, following his friend—. Don't tell me you want to go up...

—Tenemos que ir a ver! Debe ser una **paloma** o algo así.

—We have to go up and see! It has to be a pigeon or something like that.

Rafael pisó el primer **escalón** de la **escalera** del ático. Volvió a escucharse un **extraño** grito.

Rafael stepped on the first step of the attic stairs. A strange scream was heard again.

De pronto, Petunia apareció detrás de ellos gruñendo. Ambos se asustaron. Petunia **corrió** hacia la escalera y subió hacia el ático en menos de dos segundos.

Suddenly, Petunia appeared behind them, growling. They both jumped. Petunia run to the stairs and went up to the attic in less than two seconds.

—¿Qué le pasa? —preguntó Rafael.

—What's up with her? —asked Rafael.

—Dicen que los gatos pueden ver cosas sobrenaturales —dijo Pedro—. ¡Petunia! ¡Petunia, **ven aquí**!

—They say cats can see supernatural things —said Pedro—. Petunia! Petunia, come here!

La gata no volvió a aparecer.

The cat didn't show up again.

—Esto es muy raro —dijo Pedro—. Siempre viene cuando la llamo. ¡Petunia!

—This is very weird —said Pedro—. She always comes when I call her. ¡Petunia!

Lentamente, ambos comenzaron a subir.

Slowly, they both started going up.

El ático estaba completamente **oscuro**.

The attic was completely dark.

—¿Dónde está **el interruptor de la luz**? —preguntó Rafael.

—Where is the light switch? —asked Rafael.

—¡No lo sé! —dijo Pedro—. Nunca he venido aquí de noche.

—I don't know! —said Pedro—. I never came here at night.

—¡Voy a buscar el interruptor! —dijo Rafael.

—I'm going to look for the switch —said Rafael.

—¡Espera! No me dejes solo…

—Wait! Don't leave me alone...

Pedro oyó algo extraño en **un rincón**. Un grito agudo. Un **gruñido**. Sintió como le **temblaban** las rodillas. Estaba **a punto de** desmayarse…

Pedro heard something weird in a corner. A high scream. A growl. He felt how his knees were shaking. He was about to pass out…

—¡Rafa! ¡Rafa! ¿Dónde estás? Hay algo en ese rincón, ¡Rafaaaa!

—Rafa! Rafa! Where are you? There's something in that corner, Rafaaaa!

En ese momento, se encendió la luz. Rafa estaba junto a él, con la **mano** en el interruptor. En el rincón del ático, vieron el origen del escándalo...

At that moment, the lights went on. Rafa was standing next to him, with his hand on the switch. In the corner, they saw the origin of the scandal…

—¡Gatitos! —exclamó Rafa.

—Kittens! —exclaimed Rafa.

—Petunia, ¿has tenido **bebés**? —preguntó Pedro—. ¡Con razón estabas tan **gorda**!

—Petunia, had you got some babies? —asked Pedro—. That's why you were so fat!

En el **suelo**, la gata Petunia estaba recostada junto a cinco gatitos negros que lloraban. Su llanto sonaba como gritos agudos. Cuando **se acercaron**, la gata comenzó a gruñir nuevamente.

On the floor, Petunia was lying next to five black kittens who were crying. Their crying sounded like high screams. When they went near them, the cat started to growl again.

—Tranquila, tranquila. No vamos a **hacerles daño**—dijo Pedro.

—Easy, easy. We're not going to hurt them —said Pedro.

—Son **preciosos** —dijo Rafa, mientras **acariciaba** a uno de los gatitos.

—They're beautiful —said Rafa, while petting one of the kittens.

Los amigos pasaron el resto de la noche jugando con los gatitos, mientras Petunia dormía. Rafael **se encariñó** con uno de ellos, que tenía ojos verdes.

The two friends spent the rest of the night playing with the kittens, while Petunia slept. Rafael got attached to one of them that had green eyes.

—Cuando seas **más grande**, te llevaré a casa —le dijo al gatito—. Tu nombre será... ¡Fantasma!

—When you're older, I'm going to take you home —he told the kitten—. Your name will be… Ghost!

Resumen (Summary)

Pedro y Rafael están solos en la casa de Pedro, celebrando el final de las clases. Ven una película de terror y comen bocadillos. De pronto, oyen ruidos extraños que vienen del ático. Tienen mucho miedo, pero se atreven a subir. Finalmente, se encuentran con una agradable sorpresa: ¡gatitos!

Summary

Pedro and Rafael are alone at Pedro's house, celebrating the end of school. They're watching a horror film and eating snacks. Suddenly, they hear weird noises coming from the attic. They're very scared, but they dare to go up. Finally, they find a nice surprise: kittens!

Vocabulario (Vocabulary)

A little old lady - Una viejita

Dead - Muerto

To turn on - Encender

To turn off - Apagar

To be scary - Dar miedo

To complain - Quejarse

Ghost - Fantasma

To understand - Entender

Best friends - Mejores amigos

Snacks - Golosinas

Movie - Película

Ghost stories - Historias de fantasmas

Bowl - Cuenco

Sandwich - Bocadillo

Carrot - Zanahoria

Simple - Sencillo

Torch - Linterna

Chin - Mentón

Sinister - Siniestra

Sweets - Golosinas

Scared - Asustado

Floor - Piso

A bang - Un golpe

Both - Ambos

To dare - Atreverse

Cat - Gato

Right there - Ahí mismo

Water - Agua

Scream - Grito

Main characters - Protagonistas

Killer - Asesino

Living room - Sala

The police - La policía

Bird - Pájaro

The crying - El llanto

To go near - Acercarse

Pigeon - Paloma

Step - Escalón

Stairs - Escalera

Strange - Extraño

To run - Correr

Come here - Ven aquí

Dark - Oscuro

The light switch - El interruptor de la luz

A corner - Un rincón

Growl - Gruñido

To shake - Temblar

About to - A punto de

Hand - Mano

Baby - Bebé

Fat – Gordo/a

To hurt – Hacer daño

Beautiful – Precioso/a

To pet - Acariciar

To get attached - Encariñarse

Bigger - Más grande

Preguntas (Questions)

1. ¿Qué estaban celebrando los amigos?
   a. El inicio del quinto grado.
   b. El último día de clases.
   c. El primer día de invierno.

2. ¿Qué tipo de película estaban viendo?
   a. Una película de terror.
   b. Una película de golosinas.
   c. Una película sobre una casa.

3. ¿Cuál era el nombre de la gata de Rafael?

4. ¿Qué oyen en el ático?
   a. A Petunia y sus gatitos.
   b. Un asesino.
   c. Ruido y pasos.

5. ¿Dónde está Petunia cuando se asustan?

6. ¿Qué pisa Pedro cuando se asusta?

7. ¿Qué deciden hacer?
   a. Subir al ático.
   b. Llamar a la policía.
   c. Esperar a la madre de Rafael.

8. ¿Por qué Pedro no sabe dónde está el interruptor de la luz del ático?
   a. Porque no es su casa.
   b. Porque nunca fue al ático de noche.
   c. Sí sabe, pero igualmente no lo encuentra.

9. ¿De qué color son los gatitos de Petunia?

10. ¿Qué nombre le pondrá Rafael al gatito que quiere adoptar?

Questions

1. What were the two friends celebrating?
   a. The beginning of the fifth grade.
   b. The last day of school.
   c. The first day of winter.

2. What kind of movie were they watching?

    a.   A horror film.

    b.   A movie about snacks.

    c.   A movie about a house.

3. What was the name of Pedro's cat?

4. What do they hear in the attic?

    a.   Petunia and her kittens.

    b.   A killer.

    c.   Bangs and steps.

5. Where is Petunia when they get scared?

6. What does Pedro step on when he gets scared?

7. What do they decide to do?

    a.   Go up to the attic.

    b.   Call the police.

    c.   Wait for Rafael's mother.

8. Why doesn't Pedro know where the attic light switch is?

    a.   Because it isn't his house.

    b.   Because he's never been to the attic at night.

    c.   He does know, but he still can't find it.

9. What colour are Petunia's kittens?

10. How does Rafael want to name the kitten he wants to adopt?

Respuestas (Answers)

1. b

2. a

3. La gata es de Pedro, no de Rafael.

4. c

5. En la sala, tomando agua.

6. Un cuenco con bastones de zanahoria.

7. a

8. b

9. Negros.

10. Fantasma.

Answers

1. b

2. a

3. It's Pedro's cat, not Rafael's.

4. c

5. In the living room, drinking water.

6. A bowl with carrot sticks.

7. a

8. b

9. Black.

10. Ghost.

Chapter 7 – La niña que escribía historias (The girl who wrote stories)

Marcia **se despertó** cuando oyó la puerta de la casa.

Marcia woke up when she heard the front door.

Era su padre, que **volvía** de trabajar.

It was her father, who came back from work.

Su padre trabajaba **toda la noche** en un restaurante.

Her father worked all night at a restaurant.

Llegaba a la casa a las siete de la mañana y cocinaba el **desayuno** para sus hijas antes de **acostarse a dormir**.

He arrived home around seven in the morning and cooked breakfast to his daughters before going to bed.

Marcia lo estaba esperando con **impaciencia** porque quería decirle algo muy importante.

Marcia was waiting for him impatiently because she had something very important to tell him.

—¡Papá! ¡Papá! —gritó, mientras corría en pijama hacia la puerta.

—Dad! Dad! —she screamed, while she run to the door in her pajamas.

Dio a su padre un fuerte abrazo.

She gave her father a big hug.

—No vas a creer lo que vi ayer en la tele, ¡vi la **muñeca** más hermosa de *todo* el mundo! Es lo que me gustaría por mi cumpleaños… ¡por favor!

—You're not going to believe what I saw on the TV yesterday, I saw the prettiest doll in the *whole* world! It's what I'd like for my present… please!

Su padre la escuchaba con una sonrisa.

Her father was listening with a smile.

—Hija, ya lo hemos hablado muchas veces. Esas muñecas de la tele son muy **caras**. Con mi **sueldo** y el de mamá apenas nos llega para pagar todos nuestros **gastos** y **ahorrar** un poco. ¡No tenemos dinero suficiente para regalos caros!

—Girl, we've talked about this many times. Those dolls from TV are very expensive. With my salary and Mom's we barely get enough to pay for all our expenses and to save a little. We don't have enough money for expensive presents!

—Ya lo sé, papá —dijo Marcia, con tristeza—. Pero quizá **de alguna forma**…

—I know, Dad —said Marcia, sadly—. But maybe somehow…

El padre de Marcia **reflexionó**.

Marcia's father reflected.

—Cuando yo tenía tu **edad** y quería comprar algún **juguete** o alguna golosina, cocinaba galletas o **tartas** y salía a venderlas por el **barrio**. ¡Fue mi primer trabajo como **cocinero**!

—When I was your age and I wanted to buy some toy or sweet, I baked biscuits or cakes and I went out to sell them around the neighbourhood. It was my first job as a cook!

—¡Pero, papá! Yo no soy tan buena cocinando… —dijo Marcia.

—But Dad! I'm not such a good cook… —said Marcia.

—No eres mala. Pero, de todas formas, era un **ejemplo**. Ya tienes doce años, ¡casi trece! No está mal que hagas algún trabajito **de vez en cuando** para comprarte algo.

—You're not bad. But anyway, it was an example. You're twelve now, almost thirteen! It's not bad to do some little work every now and then to buy something for yourself.

—¿Y qué puedo hacer? —preguntó Marcia.

—And what can I do? —asked Marcia.

Su padre reflexionó por un momento, hasta que se le ocurrió una idea. Desapareció un momento, mientras Marcia preparaba café.

His father reflected for a second, until he came up with an idea. He disappeared for a moment, while Marcia prepared some coffee.

Al cabo de algunos minutos, el padre de Marcia volvió, **cargando** un **maletín** de plástico que parecía muy **pesado**.

After a few minutes, Marcia's father came back, carrying a plastic case that looked very heavy.

—¿Qué es eso? —preguntó Marcia, mientras hacía tostadas.

—What's that? —asked Marcia, while making toast.

—Esto… —dijo su padre, mientras apoyaba el maletín en la mesa y lo abría lentamente— ¡es mi vieja **máquina de escribir**!

—This… —said her father, while putting the case on the table and opening it slowly— is my old typewriter!

—¡Pero es **una antigüedad**! —dijo Marcia.

—But it's an antique! —said Marcia.

Su padre rió.

Her father laughed.

—Claro que sí, hija. Es una verdadera antigüedad. Pero ahora las antigüedades como esta están **de moda**.

—Of course it is, girl. It's a true antique. But now antiques like this are fashionable again.

—¿Y qué **sugieres** que haga?

—And what do you suggest me to do?

—Bueno, lo único que se puede hacer con una máquina de escribir…

—Well, the only thing you can do with a typewriter…

—¿**Escribir**?

—To write?

—¡**Claro**!

—Of course!

El día siguiente, después de la escuela, Marcia usó su **dinero** para comprar dos rollos de tinta que consiguió por unas pocas **monedas** en una vieja **tienda**.

The next day, after school, Marcia used her money to buy two ink ribbons that she obtained for a few coins in an old store.

Luego compró varios papeles y carpetas de colores y fue a su casa, donde se pasó toda la tarde creando historias fantásticas que más tarde **ofreció** a sus vecinos.

Then she bought some papers and colour folders and went home, where she spent the whole afternoon creating fantastic stories that she offered later to her neighbors.

En el barrio, los cuentos de Marcia tuvieron muchísimo éxito. Las señoras ancianas la esperaban todas las tardes con sus carpetas de colores. Dentro de las carpetas había historias de amor, de misterio y de aventuras.

In the neighbourhood, Marcia's stories were very successful. Old ladies waited for her every evening with her colour folders. Within the folders there were stories of love, mystery and adventure.

Algunas le pedían historias con **protagonistas** que tuvieran sus nombres.

Some asked for stories with main characters who had their names.

Para los más pequeños, Marcia creaba historias de piratas, de astronautas, de viajes en el tiempo y de criaturas fantásticas. Su hermana menor, Patricia, hacía las **ilustraciones**.

For the youngest, Marcia created stories of pirates, astronauts, time travels and fantastic creatures. Her younger sister, Patricia, made the illustrations.

Marcia solo **cobraba** unas pocas monedas por cada cuento, pero **poco a poco** su **hucha** comenzó a **llenarse** y los **pedidos** eran cada vez más.

Marcia only charged a few coins for each story, but, little by little, her moneybox started filling up and orders were more and more each time.

Sus vecinos coincidían en que los cuentos de Marcia eran excelentes **regalos** para amigos y familiares. La llamaban "La niña que escribe historias".

Her neighbours agreed on the fact that Marcia's stories were excellent presents for friends and family. They called her the "The Girl who Writes Stories".

Dos meses después de que su padre le diera la máquina de escribir, Marcia le llevó orgullosa su pesada **hucha**. Juntos, mientras desayunaban tortitas, contaron el dinero. ¡Tenía más que suficiente para comprarse tres muñecas como la que quería!

Two months after her father gave her the typewriter, Marcia proudly brought to him the heavy moneybox. Together, while having pancakes for breakfast, they counted the money. She had more than enough to buy three dolls like the one she wanted!

—Si quieres, mañana podemos ir al **centro comercial** a comprar tu regalo —dijo el padre de Marcia.

—If you want, we can go to the mall tomorrow and buy your present —said Marcia's father.

—¿Esa muñeca? ¡**No, gracias**! —dijo la niña—. Voy a gastar todo este dinero en **libros** de escritores como yo. ¡Y en rollos nuevos para mi máquina de escribir!

—That doll? No, thanks! —said the girl—. I'm going to spend all this money in books by other writers like me. And in new ribbons for my typewriter!

Resumen (Summary)

Marcia quiere una muñeca para su cumpleaños, pero su familia no tiene suficiente dinero para comprarla. Su padre le sugiere que haga algún trabajo para poder comprarse la muñeca ella misma. Para eso, le regala su vieja máquina de escribir. Marcia usa la máquina para escribir historias, que luego vende en el vecindario. Sus historias son tan buenas que hace mucho dinero. Pero, finalmente, ya no quiere la muñeca. Su nuevo amor es la literatura.

Summary

Marcia wants a doll for her birthday, but her family doesn't have enough money to buy it. Her father suggest her to do some work in order to buy the doll herself. For that, he gives her his old typewriter. Marcia uses the typewriter to write stories that she later sells around the neighbourhood. Her stories are so good that she makes a lot of money. But, finally, she doesn't want the doll anymore. Her new love is literature.

Vocabulario (Vocabulary)

To wake up - Despertarse

To come back - Volver

All night - Toda la noche

Breakfast - Desayuno

To go to bed - Acostarse a dormir

Impatience - Impaciencia

Doll - Muñeca

Expensive – Caro/a

Salary - Sueldo

Expenses - Gastos

To save - Ahorrar

Somehow - De alguna forma

To reflect - Reflexionar

Age - Edad

Toy - Juguete

Cake - Tarta

Neighborhood – Barrio/Vecindario

Cook - Cocinero

Example - Ejemplo

From time to time - De vez en cuando

To carry - Cargar

Case - Maletín

Heavy – Pesado/a

Typewriter - Máquina de escribir

An antique - Una antigüedad

Fashionable - De moda

To suggest - Sugerir

To write - Escribir

Of course! - ¡Claro!

Money - Dinero

Coins - Monedas

Store - Tienda

To offer - Ofrecer

Main character - Protagonista

Illustration - Ilustración

To charge - Cobrar

Little by little - Poco a poco

Moneybox - Hucha

To fill up - Llenarse

Order - Pedido

Present - Regalo

Mall - Centro comercial

No, thanks - No, gracias

Book – Libro

Preguntas (Questions)

1. ¿Por qué el padre de Marcia llega a la casa por la mañana?

    a. No llega por la mañana; llega por la noche.
    b. Porque es cocinero.
    c. Porque trabaja por la noche.

2. ¿Qué importante anuncio tiene que hacer Marcia a su padre?

    a. Que ya sabe qué quiere para su cumpleaños.
    b. Que quiere una máquina de escribir.
    c. Que se ha comprado una muñeca.

3. ¿Qué objeto regala su padre a Marcia?

4. ¿Qué compra Marcia al día siguiente?

    a. Una máquina de escribir.
    b. Una muñeca.
    c. Rollos de tinta, papeles y carpetas.

5. ¿Dónde vendía Marcia sus historias?

6. ¿Qué le pedían algunas señoras del barrio?

7. ¿Quién hacía las ilustraciones de las historias de Marcia?

    a. Su hermana.
    b. Patricia, su madre.
    c. Su hermana mayor.

8. ¿Cómo la llaman en el barrio?

    a. La chica que cuenta cuentos.
    b. La niña que escribe historias.
    c. La niña que escribía historias.

9. ¿Cuánto dinero obtiene Marcia?

10. ¿Qué quiere ir a comprar Marcia al centro comercial?

Questions

1. Why does Marcia's father arrive home early in the morning?

    a. He doesn't arrive in the morning; he gets home at night.
    b. Because he's a cook.
    c. Because he works during the night.

2. What important announcement does Marcia want to make to her father?

    a.   That she already knows what she wants for her birthday.
    b.   That she wants a typewriter.
    c.   That she bought a doll.

3. What object does Marcia get from her father?

4. What does Marcia buy the next day?

    a.   A typewriter.
    b.   A doll.
    c.   Ink ribbons, papers and folders.

5. Where did Marcia sell her stories?

6. What did some ladies from the neighbourhood asked her for?

7. Who made the illustrations for Marcia's stories?

    a.   Her sister.
    b.   Patricia, her mother.
    c.   Her older sister.

8. What do they call Marcia in the neighbourhood?

    a.   The Girl who Tells Tales.
    b.   The Girl who Writes Stories.
    c.   The Girl who Wrote Stories.

9. How much money did Marcia obtain?

10. What does Marcia want to buy at the mall?

Respuestas (Answers)

1. c

2. a

3. Una máquina de escribir.

4. c

5. En su barrio.

6. Pedían personajes que tuvieran sus nombres.

7. a

8. b

9. Suficiente para comprar tres muñecas como la que quería.

10. Libros y rollos de tinta.

Answers

1. c

2. a

3. A typewriter.

4. c

5. In her neighbourhood.

6. They asked for characters who had their names.

7. a

8. b

9. Enough to buy three dolls like the one she wanted.

10. Books and ink ribbons.

Chapter 8 – El rey del callejón (The king of the alley)

Nadie me cree cuando cuento que en mi **país**, Bolivia, las cosas no son como en todos lados. Las **nubes** son mágicas y los animales hablan.

Nobody believes me when I tell them that in my country, Bolivia, things are not as everywhere else. Clouds are magical, and animals can talk.

Un día, cuando era un joven **escritor**, estaba caminando bajo la peor **tormenta** que había visto en años. Estaba pensando en una nueva historia para escribirla.

One day, when I was a young writer, I was walking under the worst storm I had seen in years. I was thinking of a new story to write.

"Otro **día soleado**", dije con sarcasmo, mirando al cielo.

"Another sunny day", I thought sarcastically, looking up to the sky.

Las nubes me oyeron, evidentemente. Al instante, lanzaron sobre mí una dura **lluvia** de **tornillos**.

The clouds heard me, evidently. Right then, they dropped on me a hard rain of screws.

"Preferiría **algo para comer**", dije, con **enfado**.

"I'd rather something to eat", I said, angrily.

En ese instante, comenzó a caer sobre mí una tormenta de cubos de **queso**.

Right then, a cheese cube storm started falling on my head.

No podía caminar ni mirar hacia adelante, así que tuve que esconderme.

I could neither walk nor look ahead, so I had to hide.

A mi derecha había **un angosto callejón**, el más angosto de la ciudad.

To my right there was a narrow alley, the narrowest in town.

De hecho, el callejón era tan angosto que las nubes me **perdieron de vista**.

The alley was so narrow that the clouds lost the sight of me.

Comencé a caminar por el callejón… o, **al menos,** lo intenté.

I started walking down the alley, or at least I tried to.

El espacio entre las paredes era tan escaso y estaba tan lleno de **cajas**, **basura** y otros objetos que apenas podía poner un **pie** frente al otro.

The space between the walls was so little and so full of boxes, trash and other objects that I could barely put one feet in front of the other.

Por suerte todavía no era un escritor **exitoso**, por lo que era mucho más **delgado** que ahora. No creo que fuera físicamente posible que entrara en ese callejón **ahora**, con mi gran **barriga**.

I was lucky that I wasn't a successful writer yet, so I was much thinner than I am now. I don't think it would be physically possible for me to fit into that alley now, with my big belly.

Incluso si pudiera entrar en ese callejón, no volvería a hacerlo… ni por todo el **dinero** del mundo.

Even if I could fit into that alley, I wouldn't do it… for all the money in the world.

Lo que encontré ese día en el fondo del callejón fue tan **terrorífico** que prometí que nunca volvería a poner un pie en él.

What I found that day in its end was so terrifying that I promised I wouldn't put a foot in there again.

—Esos dos **trozos** de **carne** que tienes ahí se ven deliciosos—, dijo **una voz grave** desde lo más profundo del callejón.

—Those two pieces of meat you have there look delicious—, said a deep voice from the deepest end of the alley.

Me detuve. Podía oír los **latidos** de mi corazón.

I stopped. I could hear my own heartbeat.

—Ho… Hola —dije—, ¿Hay alguien aquí?.

—He… Hello —I said—, Is there anyone here?.

Nadie respondió.

No one answered.

Comencé a caminar nuevamente, muy **despacio**.

I started walking again, very slowly.

—Me gusta que vengan **visitas** a mi callejón —dijo la voz—, especialmente cuando tienen pies grandes y olorosos como los tuyos.

—I like visitors coming into my alley —said the voice—, especially when they have big smelly feet like yours.

No podía ver quién hablaba.

I couldn't see who was speaking.

Miré a mi alrededor y todo lo que podía ver eran pilas de basura y cajas vacías.

I looked around and all I could see were piles of smelly rubbish and empty boxes.

De pronto, la voz lanzó una fuerte carcajada a mi derecha. Me di la vuelta.

Suddenly, the voice laughed out loud to my right. I turned.

Había una **maceta** vacía colgando de la **pared**. Dentro de ella, una rata gigantesca estaba sentada cómodamente.

There was an empty flower pot hanging from the wall. Inside of it, an enormous rat was sitting comfortably.

Sobre su **cabeza**, tenía una **lata de cerveza** vacía a modo de **corona**.

On top of its head, it had an empty beer can as a crown.

En su mano derecha, sostenía una vieja **cuchara** de madera como un cetro.

On his right hand, it was holding an old wooden spoon as a scepter.

—Soy el **rey** Diego —dijo la rata—. Soy el jefe de este callejón.

—I am King Diego —said the rat—. I am the chief of this alley.

—Ah… —dije, algo **confundido**—. **Discúlpeme**. Me iré de inmediato, su Majestad.

—Oh… —I said, confused— Forgive me. I will leave immediately, Your Majesty.

—No lo harás—, dijo la rata.

—You won't—, said the rat.

Miré a mi alrededor. ¡Estaba rodeado! Todo tipo de **ratas y ratones** me rodeaban. Sostenían **tenedores y cuchillos**.

I looked around. I was surrounded! All kinds of rats and mice were surrounding me. They were holding forks and knives.

Intenté correr, pero tropecé con una cáscara de **sandía** y me caí sobre el pavimento mojado.

I tried to run, but I tripped on a watermelon rind and fell on the wet pavement.

De pronto, estaban sobre mí.

Suddenly, they were all over me.

Me **ataron** como a Gulliver.

They tied me down like Gulliver.

Alcé la vista y vi al rey Diego frente a mí.

I looked up and I saw King Diego in front of me

—Como dije —repitió—, me gustan las visitas, especialmente con pies como los tuyos. Por supuesto que nos gustaría comer algo de queso de vez en cuando, pero debemos conformarnos con pies que *huelen a queso*…

—Like I said —he repeated—, I really like visitors, especially with feet like yours. Of course we would love to eat some cheese every now and then, but we have to settle with feet that *smell like cheese*…

—¿ESTÁS DICIENDO QUE VAN A COMERSE MIS PIES?—, exclamé.

—DO YOU MEAN YOU ARE GOING TO EAT MY FEET?—, I exclaimed.

Sentí que me iba a **desmayar**.

I felt I was about to pass out.

Los roedores se acercaban cada vez más a mis botas de agua.

The rodents were coming closer and closer to my rain boots.

Por mi **frente** rodaban **gotas** de sudor más grandes que las gotas de la tormenta de algunos minutos atrás… —¡Eso es!, pensé.

Down my forehead rolled drops of sweat bigger than the drops of the storm from some minutes ago… —That's it!—, I thought.

—¡Queso! —**grité**—. ¡TENGO QUESO!

—Cheese! —I shouted—. I HAVE CHEESE!

Las ratas y los ratones se detuvieron, confundidos.

The rats and mice stopped, confused.

El rey Diego me habló:

King Diego addressed me:

—¿*Queso* dices?.

—*Cheese* you say?.

—Sí —contesté—. Puedo **conseguir** mucho queso en menos de un minuto.

—Yes —I replied—. I can get a lot of cheese in less than a minute.

Los roedores parecían interesados.

The rodents seemed interested.

—Te prometo que si me **sueltan** conseguiré un montón de queso en un instante.

—I promise you that if you let me go I'll get you a ton of cheese this instant.

El rey Diego dudaba. No confiaba en mí, pero él y sus súbditos preferían la promesa de queso que la **certeza** de los pies delgados, sucios y mojados de un escritor.

King Diego doubted. He didn't trust me, but he and his subjects preferred the promise of cheese than the certainty of skinny, dirty wet writer's feet.

Dio la orden.

He gave the order.

En menos de tres segundos, estaba libre.

In less than three seconds, I was free.

Me puse de pie y, lentamente, fui hacia la pared.

I stood up and, slowly, moved towards the wall.

Comencé a **trepar** sobre las cajas hasta que llegué a una **escalera** de incendios.

I started climbing boxes until I reached a fire escape ladder.

—¿Dónde crees que vas?—, preguntó Diego.

—Where do you think you are going?—, asked Diego.

—**Confía** en mí —le dije—. Tendrás tu queso.

—Trust me —I said—. You'll get your cheese.

Comencé a subir lo más rápido posible. Las ratas me seguían. Cuando llegué al techo, miré hacia el cielo y grité:

I started going up as fast as I could. Rats were following me. When I reached the rooftop, I looked up to the sky and shouted:

—¡Aquí estoy! ¡Aquí estoy! ¿Esa es la lluvia más fuerte que tienen?—

—Here I am1 Here I am! Is that the heaviest rain you have?—

Tan pronto como las nubes me vieron, se apresuraron sobre mí.

As soon as the clouds saw me, they rushed over me.

Unos segundos después, una tempestad de queso y tornillos caía sobre y mí y sobre el callejón.

A few seconds later, a tempest of cheese and screws was falling over me and into the alley.

Los roedores estaban más **felices** que nunca, excepto por uno o dos que se **tragaron** un tornillo.

The rodents were happier than ever, except for one or two who swallowed a screw.

Mientras escapaba por los techos, **me di la vuelta** una última vez. El callejón estaba casi **repleto** de queso. El rey Diego navegaba sobre él, riendo. Su bote era una caja de cartón y su **remo** era su vieja cuchara de madera.

While I escaped on the roofs, I turned one last time. The alley was almost filled with cheese. King Diego was sailing on it, while laughing. His boat was a cardboard box and his row was his old wooden spoon.

Resumen (Summary)

Un joven escritor huye de una lluvia mágica. Se esconde en un callejón, donde una gran rata y sus amigas se quieren comer sus pies. Sin embargo, él tiene algo mejor para ofrecerles: ¡una lluvia de queso!

Summary

A young writer runs away from a magical storm. He hides inside an alley, where a big rat and its friends want to eat his feet. However, he has something better to offer them: a rain of cheese!

Vocabulario (Vocabulary)

Country - País

Clouds - Nubes

Writer – Escritor/a

Storm - Tormenta

Sunny day - Día soleado

Rain - Lluvia

Screw - Tornillo

Something to eat - Algo para comer

Anger - Endado

Cheese - Queso

A narrow alley - Un callejón angosto

To lose of sight - Perder de vista

At least - Al menos

Box - Caja

Trash - Basura

Foot - Pie

Luckily - Por suerte

Successful - Exitoso

Thin – Delgado/a

Now - Ahora

Belly - Barriga

Even if - Incluso si

Money - Dinero

Terrifying - Terrorífico

Piece - Trozo

Meat - Carne

A deep voice - Una voz grave

Heartbeat - Latido

Slowly - Despacio

Visitors - Visitas

Flower pot - Maceta

Wall - Muro

Head - Cabeza

Beer can - Lata de cerveza

Crown - Corona

Spoon - Cuchara

King - Rey

Confused - Confundido

Forgive me - Discúlpeme

Rats and mice - Ratas y ratones

Forks and knives - Tenedores y cuchillos

Watermelon - Sandía

To tie - Atar

To smell - Oler

To pass out - Desmayarse

Drop - Gota

Forehead - Frente

To shout - Gritar

To get - Conseguir

To let go - Soltar

Certainty - Certeza

To climb - Trepar

Ladder - Escalera

To trust - Confiar

Happy - Feliz

Swallow - Tragar

To turn around – Darse la vuelta

Full - Repleto

Row – Remo

Preguntas (Questions)

1. ¿Cuál es la profesión del narrador?

    a. Trepador.
    b. Notario.
    c. Escritor.

2. ¿Qué está haciendo mientras camina por la calle?

    a. Piensa en una historia para escribir.
    b. Escribe.
    c. Narra.

3. ¿Por qué se esconde en el callejón?

4. ¿Qué le arrojan las nubes?

    a. Tornillos.
    b. Cubos de queso.
    c. Opciones a y b.

5. ¿Con qué famoso personaje de la literatura se compara el narrador cuando las ratas lo atan?

6. ¿Qué quieren hacer las ratas con él?

7. ¿Cómo logra que las ratas lo liberen?

    a. Les ofrece algo mejor que sus pies.
    b. ˙ Les ofrece algo peor que sus pies.
    c. Les ofrece hablar con las nubes.

8. ¿Cómo llega el narrador al techo?

    a. Caminando.
    b. Trepando.
    c. Navegando.

9. ¿Está contento El rey Diego al final de la historia?

10. ¿Qué usa el rey Diego para remar?

Questions

1. What's the narrator's profession?

    a. Climber.
    b. Notary.
    c. Writer.

2. What's he doing while he walks on the street?

a. He's thinking of a story to write.
b. He's writing.
c. He's narrating.

3. Why does he hide in the alley?

4. What are the clouds dropping on him?

a. Screws.
b. Cheese cubes.
c. Options a and b.

5. With what famous fictional character does the narrator compares himself when rats tie him down?

6. What do the rats want to do with him?

7. How does he get the rats to release him?

a. He offers them something better than his feet.
b. He offers them something worse than his feet.
c. He offers them to talk to the clouds.

8. How does the narrator get to the rooftop?

a. Walking.
b. Climbing.
c. Navigating.

9. Is King Diego happy at the end of the story?

10. What does King Diego use to row?

Respuestas (Answers)

1. c

2. a

3. Porque las nubes están arrojando una tormenta de queso sobre él.

4. c

5. Gulliver.

6. Quieren comerse sus pies.

7. a

8. b

9. Sí.

10. Una vieja cuchara de madera.

Answers

1. c

2. a

3. Because the clouds are dropping a magical cheese storm on him.

4. c

5. Gulliver.

6. They want to eat his feet.

7. a

8. b

9. Yes.

10. An old wooden spoon.

Chapter 9 – Caminata hacia Cabo Polonio

Mi aventura comenzó cuando mi editor, hace dos semanas, me propuso que **escribiera un artículo** sobre una ciudad *slow*. Inmediatamente, pensé en Cabo Polonio. Hacía mucho tiempo quería ir allí.

My adventure started two weeks ago, when my editor proposed that I wrote an article on a — slow— town. I immediately thought of Cabo Polonio. I had wanted to get there for a long time.

Si usted, querido lector, no sabe lo que es una ciudad *slow*, le contaré: se trata de una ciudad (en este caso, un pueblo) sin **electricidad**, sin grandes construcciones, sin internet… en definitiva, un sitio ideal para **desconectarse** de la vida rápida y agitada que llevamos **día a día**.

If you, dear reader, don't know what a —slow— city is, I'll tell you: it's a city (in this case, a small town) without electrical power, without big buildings, without internet access… In short, it's an ideal place to disconnect from the fast and agitated life we live day after day.

Cabo Polonio, o eso creía, era un hermoso **paraíso** en la costa del Uruguay, donde me esperaba una **paz** inaudita. A este lugar maravilloso, según había leído, solo podía llegarse en un transporte especial o caminando desde la ciudad cercana de Valizas. No se podía **llegar en coche**.

Cabo Polonio, or so I thought, was a beautiful paradise in the coast of Uruguay, where an unheard peace was waiting for me. You could only reach this marvellous place, so I'd read, using special transportation means or walking from the nearby city of Valizas. You couldn't get there by car.

Por supuesto, **una caminata al atardecer** hacia este oasis de tranquilidad parecía **la mejor opción**.

Of course, a sunset walk towards this tranquility oasis sounded like the best option.

Partí desde Buenos Aires en ferri, junto con mi fiel bicicleta. Bajamos en Colonia, donde pude disfrutar de una hermosa tarde sobre sus **calles adoquinadas**, sus cafés pintorescos y su hermosa gente.

I departed from Buenos Aires on a ferry, together with my loyal bicycle. We got down at Colonia, where I could enjoy a lovely afternoon on its cobbled streets, its picturesque coffee shops and its beautiful people.

Después, comencé a pedalear. Pasé por las playas de Piriápolis; por la bella y activa ciudad de Montevideo, con sus murgas y sus fiestas; pasé por la hermosa **laguna** de Rocha; hasta que **por fin** llegué a **mi destino**: Valizas.

Then, I started pedaling. I went through Piriápolis beaches; through the beautiful and active city of Montevideo, with its *murgas* and its parties, I went through the beautiful Rocha lagoon; until finally I arrived to my destination: Valizas.

En Valizas, **pasé la noche** en un colorido hostal, donde guardé mi bicicleta. Era **un viaje** que debía hacer solo. —No te preocupes, vuelvo mañana—, le dije a la bici. Después de comer un rico almuerzo, partí hacia Cabo Polonio.

In Valizas, I spent the night in a colourful hostel, where I put away my bicycle. It was a trip I had to do by myself. —Don't worry, I'll be back tomorrow—, I told the bike. After having a good brunch, I departed towards Cabo Polonio.

La **caminata** fue una de las mejores que hice en mi vida. Se trata de **un trayecto** de unas seis horas a pie por la playa. El paisaje dorado era eterno.

The hike was one of the best I ever did in my life. It's a six hour foot journey on the beach. The golden landscape was eternal.

Por momentos, el suelo era plano y sólido, pero en algunas partes se convertía en altas dunas de arena suelta, sobre las que era difícil apoyar los pies. **Recomiendo** llevar un buen par de zapatillas (o *championes*, como les dicen en Uruguay).

At times, the ground was flat and solid, but at some parts, it turned into tall dunes of loose sand, on top of which it was difficult to set foot on. I recommend using a good pair of sneakers (or *championes*, as they call them here in Uruguay).

En el camino me encontré con varios **grupos de viajeros**, algunos que iban y otros que volvían. Casi siempre era **gente joven**.

On the way, I ran into many groups of travellers, some who went and some who came back. It was mainly young people.

Pero me encontré con otra cosa además de la gente. Me encontré algo que me hizo sentir por momentos que me encontraba dentro de un cuadro surrealista…

But I ran into something else other than people. I ran into something that made me feel at times that I was inside a surrealist painting…

La marea llevaba a esas playas todos sus **desechos**. Me encontré con **bellezas** insólitas, como viejas botellas de vidrio con mejillones creciendo dentro y fuera (tenía la esperanza de que alguna contuviera un mensaje), esqueletos de pescados, botes de madera rotos y mucho más. Lo más alucinante que vi fue una gigantesca tortuga muerta. Con su caparazón, tenía casi mi altura. Cuando la vi **en la distancia** no sabía lo que era, solo podía distinguir **un grupo de gente** reunido a su alrededor. Todos la observaban en silencio. Tenía una expresión pacífica en el **rostro**, como si hubiera muerto feliz. Al igual que con las botellas, sobre su caparazón crecía **una increíble cantidad** de moluscos… Con toda esa vida creciendo sobre ella, era difícil creer que realmente estuviera muerta.

The tide took all its trash to those beaches. I found unusual beauties, such as old glass bottles with mussels growing in and out of them (I hoped that some had a message), fish bones, broken wooden boats and much more. The most amazing thing I saw was a dead gigantic sea turtle. With its shell, it was almost mi height. When I saw it from a distance, I didn't know what it was, I could only distinguish a group of people gathered around it. They all watched it in silence. It had a peaceful expression on its face, as if it had died happily. Just like with the bottles, on its shell there was a great amount of mollusks… With all that life growing on it, it was difficult to believe that it was really dead.

Después de contemplarla un rato, seguí mi camino.

After contemplating it for a while, I continued my journey.

Ya estaba **a menos de una hora** del lugar prometido.

I was less that an hour away from the promised place.

Fue entonces cuando el sol comenzó a descender. **El atardecer** se veía alucinante sobre el océano. Todo se tiñó de un increíble tono **dorado** que cubría por igual **el cielo**, **el mar** y **la arena**.

It was then when the sun started going down. Sunset looked great on the ocean. It was all coloured with an incredible golden tone that covered equally the sky, the sea and the sand.

De pronto, de un segundo a otro, era de noche. Ya estaba **por llegar**. Pero vi algo que me sorprendió: Cabo Polonio (supuestamente sin luz eléctrica) estaba lleno de luces. Se las veía como una constelación desde la distancia.

Suddenly, from one second to the other, it was nighttime. I was about to arrive. But I saw something that surprised me: Cabo Polonio (supposedly a town without electrical power) was full of lights. You could see them like a constellation from a distance.

Sin embargo, mi confusión se aclaró cuando llegué al pueblo. No se trataba de luces eléctricas: ¡lo que se veía desde la distancia eran **velas**!

However, my confusion was clarified when I arrived to the town. It wasn't electric lights: what you could see from a distance were candles!

En el pueblo la gente se agrupaba en pintorescos cafés iluminados por velas. La gente tomaba vino y comía. Todos **charlaban** tranquilamente. Me senté en uno de estos locales y, **agotado**, me pedí una botella de Malbec y una potente **cena**. Pregunté al dueño del restaurante sobre la posibilidad de **conseguir una cama donde dormir** esa noche, pero me dijo que sería muy difícil a esa hora. Generalmente la gente **reservaba con semanas o meses de anticipación** y solía estar **todo completo**.

In the village, people gathered at picturesque coffee shops illuminated by candle lights. People had wine and ate. Everybody chatted peacefully. I sat by one of those stores and, exhausted, I ordered a bottle of Malbec and a potent meal. I asked the owner about the possibility of getting a bed to sleep on that night, but he told me it would be very difficult at that time. Generally, people booked weeks or months in advance and everything was usually booked.

No me preocupé demasiado. Era una noche cálida y llevaba conmigo mi **bolsa de dormir**. Por eso, después de pagar, me dirigí a la playa.

I didn't worry too much. It was a warm night and I had my sleeping bag with me. So, after paying, I went to the beach.

Me acosté sobre la arena y miré el cielo durante un rato largo, hasta que noté que las **estrellas** desaparecían bajo un manto gris. Era una enorme nube. A los pocos minutos, comenzaron a caer las primeras gotas y, unos instantes después, caía sobre mí la peor **tormenta** que hubiera podido imaginar.

I layed down on the sand and looked up to the sky for a long while, until I noticed the stars were disappearing under a grey cover. It was an enormous cloud. A few minutes after, the first drops started falling and, a few instants later, the worst storm I could ever imagine was falling on me.

Desesperado, salí corriendo y me refugié bajo un puesto **salvavidas**. Había un espacio de menos de un metro entre la arena y la construcción de **madera**.

Desperately, I ran away and found cover under a lifeguard shack. There was less than a meter of space between the sand and the wooden construction.

Pero parece que no solo yo estaba durmiendo en la playa. Y no solo a mí me **pilló por sorpresa** la tormenta. En el momento en el que llegué a mi refugio, llegaron conmigo dos chicas que venían corriendo bajo la lluvia. Un minuto después, llegó un grupo de tres **mochileros** irlandeses. Y al cabo de diez minutos éramos más de diez personas allí debajo. Debimos amontonarnos para dormir, porque realmente no entrábamos todos, pero lo logramos. Yo tenía mis piernas sobre uno de los irlandeses y mi cabeza apoyada sobre una chica venezolana.

But it looks like I wasn't the only one sleeping on the beach. And I wasn't the only one caught by surprise by the storm. When I arrived to my refuge, two girls who were running under the rain arrived with me. A minute later, a group of three Irish backpackers arrived. And, ten minutes, later we were more than ten people under there. We had to pile up to sleep, because we really didn't fit, but we made it. I had my legs on top of one of the Irish guys and my head on a Venezuelan girl.

Si bien pasamos frío y la lluvia nos mojó bastante, fue una noche de lo más divertida. Todos contamos historias, chistes. Incluso alguien contó una **receta** de cocina. Al final, nos quedamos en silencio y dormimos **un par de horas**.

Even if we were cold and the rain got us quite wet, it was a hilarious night. We all told stories, jokes, and someone even shared a cooking recipe. At the end, we remained silent and we slept for a couple of hours.

Cuando desperté, no pude evitar sentir **una gran decepción**.

When I woke up, I couldn't help to feel a great disappointment.

El paraíso que se suponía que era Cabo Polonio no era más que una playa **sucia** y gris. La tormenta había llevado hojas y ramas a la arena. El mar estaba revuelto y el cielo se veía triste. Además, no había nadie en la playa.

The paradise Cabo Polonio was supposed to be was no more than a dirty and grey beach. The storm had thrown leaves and branches on the sand. The sea was rough and the sky looked sad. On top of that, there was nobody on the beach.

Me sentí **engañado** por mis **expectativas**.

I felt fooled by my expectations.

Sin embargo, me senté a **leer un libro** sobre la arena.

However, I sat to read a book on the sand.

Al cabo de un rato, levanté la vista y vi que **el paisaje** había comenzado a cambiar: el sol comenzaba a brillar; el cielo se ponía azul; llegaban los primeros turistas. Di **un paseo** por el pueblo, donde estaban abriendo las tiendas pequeñas. Al cabo de un rato, volví a la playa, ahora **llena de vida**, radiante y blanca.

After a while, I looked up and saw the landscape had started to change: the sun was starting to shine; the sky was turning blue; the first tourists arrived. I walked around town, where the little shops were opening. After a while, I returned to the beach, now full of life, radiant and white.

Finalmente, encontré mi paraíso. A veces hay que dar algo de tiempo después de una tormenta.

Finally, I found my paradise. Sometimes you have to give it some time after a storm.

En la playa, encontré a algunos de los jóvenes con los que había pasado la noche anterior. Nos sentamos en círculo. Algunos tenían guitarras. Tomamos mate al estilo uruguayo, cantamos canciones, contamos historias y, cuando comenzó la tarde, volvimos todos caminando a Valizas.

At the beach, I found some of the young people with whom I had spent the night before. We sat on a round. Some had guitars. We had Uruguayan style *mate* tea, sang songs, told stories and, when the afternoon arrived, we all walked back to Valizas together.

Resumen (Summary)

Un joven periodista viaja a Uruguay desde Buenos Aires para escribir un artículo sobre la ciudad *slow,* Cabo Polonio. Va en bicicleta desde Colonia hasta Valizas, desde donde camina hasta su destino final. Cuando llega allí, no encuentra un lugar para dormir, por lo que duerme en la playa, pero una terrible tormenta comienza. Encuentra un refugio, que tiene que compartir con muchas otras personas. Al día siguiente, la playa no se ve nada bien, pero después de un rato el clima mejora y la gente anima el lugar, por lo que finalmente encuentra su paraíso *slow*.

Summary

A young journalist travels to Uruguay from Buenos Aires to write a story on the slow town of Cabo Polonio. He cycles from Colonia to Valizas, from where he walks to his final destination. When he gets there, he doesn't find a pace to sleep, so he sleeps on the beach, but a terrible storm starts. He finds a refuge, which he has to share with a bunch of other people. The next day, the beach doesn't look very good, but after a while, the weather gets better and the people cheers up the place, so he finally finds his —slow— paradise.

Vocabulario (Vocabulary)

To write an article - Escribir un artículo

Electrical power - Electricidad

To disconnect from- Desconectarse

Day after day - Día a día

Paradise - Paraíso

Peace - Paz

To arrive by car - Llegar en auto

A walk at sunset - Una caminata al atardecer

The best choice - La mejor opción

Cobbled streets - Calles adoquinadas

Lagoon - Laguna

Finally - Por fin

My destination - Mi destino

To spend the night - Pasar la noche

A trip - Un viaje

A walk - Una caminata

A journey - Un trayecto

To recommend - Recomendar

A group of travellers - Un grupo de viajeros

Young people - Gente joven

Waste - Desechos

Beauty - Belleza

From a distance - En la distancia

A group of people - Un grupo de gente

Face - Rostro

An incredible amount - Una increíble cantidad

Less than an hour away - A menos de una hora

Sunset - Atardecer

Golden - Dorado

The sky - El cielo

The sea - El mar

The sand - La arena

About to arrive - por llegar

Candles - Velas

To chat - Charlar

Exhausted - Agotado

Dinner - Cena

To get a bed to sleep on - Conseguir una cama donde dormir

To book weeks or months in advance - Reservar con semanas o meses de anticipación

All booked - Todo completo

Sleeping bag - Bolsa de dormir

Stars - Estrellas

Storm - Tormenta

Lifeguard – Salvavidas

Wood - Madera

To take by surprise - Pillar por sorpresa

Backpackers - Mochileros

Recipe - Receta

A couple of hours - Un par de horas

A great disappointment - Una gran decepción

Dirty - Sucio

Fooled - Engañado

Expectations - Expectativas

To read a book - Leer un libro

The landscape - El paisaje

A walk - Un paseo

Full of life - Lleno de vida

Preguntas (Questions)

1. ¿De quién fue la idea de que el narrador fuera de viaje?

   a. Fue su idea.

   b. Fue idea de un periodista.

   c. Fue idea de su editor.

2. ¿Qué es un pueblo *slow*?

   a. Un pueblo donde los automóviles van despacio.

   b. Un pueblo donde no hay comida rápida.

   c. Un pueblo sin electricidad ni internet.

3. ¿Cómo se puede llegar a Cabo Polonio?

4. ¿Cómo llega el narrador hasta Uruguay?

   a. En bicicleta.

   b. En ferri.

   c. Caminando.

5. ¿Dónde deja su bicicleta cuando parte hacia Cabo Polonio?

6. ¿Qué recomienda a sus lectores para la caminata?

7. ¿Qué encontró en el camino hacia Cabo Polonio?

   a. Botellas con moluscos, una tortuga muerta y esqueletos de pescados.

   b. Botellas de vidrio con mensajes dentro.

   c. Un buen par de zapatillas.

8. ¿Por qué se veían muchas luces en Cabo Polonio?

   a. Porque sí había luz eléctrica.

   b. Era una constelación.

   c. Eran velas.

9. ¿Dónde durmió el narrador?

10. ¿Volvió solo a Valizas?

Questions

1. Whose idea was it that the narrator went on a trip?

   a. It was his idea.

   b. It was a journalist's idea.

   c. It was his editor's idea.

2. What is a —slow— town?

a. A town where all the cars drive slowly.

b. A town where there is no fast food.

c. A town without electrical power and Internet.

3. How can you get to Cabo Polonio?

4. How does the narrator get to Uruguay?

a. Cycling.

b. By ferry.

c. On foot.

5. Where does he leave his bicycle when he goes to Cabo Polonio?

6. What does he recommend to his readers for the hike?

7. What did he find on the way to Cabo Polonio?

a. Bottles with molluscs, a dead turtle and fish bones.

b. Glass bottles with messages inside of them.

c. A good pair of shoes.

8. Why many lights could be seen at Cabo Polonio?

a. Because finally there was electrical power.

b. It was a constellation.

c. They were candles.

9. Where did the narrator sleep?

10. Did he return to Valizas alone?

Respuestas (Answers)

1. c

2. c

3. Usando un transporte especial o caminando.

4. b

5. En un hostal en Valizas.

6. Llevar un buen par de zapatillas.

7. a

8. c

9. Bajo un puesto de salvavidas.

10. No, vuelve con un grupo de jóvenes que conoció la noche anterior.

Answers

1. c

2. c

3. Using a special transportation or walking.

4. b

5. In a hostel in Valizas.

6. To take a good pair of sneakers.

7. a

8. c

9. Under a lifeguard shack.

10. No, he walks back with a group of friends he made the night before.

Conclusion

Congratulations, dear reader!

We hope you had fun reading our stories, because we had fun writing them! We congratulate you for reaching the end of this book. We hope that through our pages, you found everything you expected and more, especially if your main goal was to get better in your second language while having fun and reading simple, captivating and interesting stories.

Now that you proved to yourself that you were able to read and to understand our fiction book (with the aid of our translations, summaries, vocabulary sections and questions) you are more prepared to travel, engage in conversations with people from Latin America and Spain and test your Spanish skills in real-life situations.

We truly hope these tales and what you learned from them sticks with you. As we said in the introduction section of this book, it is so natural for humans to tell stories that it's something that exists and has existed in all cultures and every moment of history, without exceptions. Nonetheless, it is not just universal that we tell stories but also the fact that we listen to them… or read them, as in this situation.

Without a spectator, the production of fiction is worthless. It is necessary that someone is willing to provide two eyes and some of their time to walk into the imaginary world that the narrator creates and to get lost in its universe.

For this reason, we want to thank you kindly. Thank you for lending us your attention and your effort.

We hope you enjoyed this nine-story trip! We hope we inspired you to travel, to read more and to keep on studying! We definitely hope you come back again to these stories whenever you feel like stepping away from routine and wandering into our imagined scenarios.

Until our next book!"

If you enjoyed this book, can you please leave a review for it?

Thanks for your support!

Part 3: Spanish Phrase Book

The Ultimate Spanish Phrase Book for Travelers of Spain or South America, Including Over 1000 Phrases for Accommodations, Eating, Traveling, Shopping, and More

Introduction

¡Hola!

Spanish is very special, since it's the official language of 20 countries and around 400 million people speak it. Not only it's one of the most spoken languages in the world, but Spanish is also one of the most studied… by people like you!

Even if you've studied Spanish before, nothing will give you the vocabulary you need to be really fluent like travelling around Latin America and Spain. But for this, you need the perfect companion, the travel book that will guide you through all kinds of activities. As you read *and* use the vocabulary and the phrases we will provide you with, they will settle in your memory and you'll find yourself, after some time, completely fluent.

Even if improvising a sign language is always an option, communicating with the locals the right way will allow you to learn Spanish appropriately, so it can become a proper asset for your work, studies, social life and many other spheres of your life. And it can really be an asset, since so many people speak and study this language nowadays, even in the corporate and academic worlds. On top of that, having friends in Latin America or Spain is something you'll never regret if you love travelling. And how about a Spanish-speaking romance?

Once you're fluent in Spanish, you'll find access to a whole new cultural world. For example, you'll be able to read books in Spanish that are not yet translated to your language, or you'll be able to pop into any cinema in Latin America and enjoy a good local movie without subtitles.

This phrase-book can actually give you the tools to communicate effectively and fit into the Spanish-speaking world so you can achieve all this.

All the former being said, we encourage you to use this book but also to travel, to immerse yourself in the Spanish-speaking cultures, to read fiction and newspapers in Spanish, to watch films, to eat Latin American and Spanish food and learn the recipes, to make Spanish-speaking friends and, most importantly, to enjoy all this. Because learning a new language and becoming fluent should always be fun, even if (or because) you will make some mistakes on the way.

We hope you really have fun using this book!

¡Buena suerte!

Chapter 1 - Pronunciation

Spanish pronunciation is really simple in comparison to other languages. The Spanish alphabet contains 27 letters, most of which are pronounced in only one way. Nonetheless, there are a few exceptions, which we will cover in this section.

Vowels

Letter *a* is always pronounced as the *a* in *apricot*. You will find this sound in words like *casa* (*house*).

Letter *e* is always pronounced as the *e* in *elephant*. You will find this sound in words like *verde* (*green*).

Letter *i* always sounds like the *i* in *intelligence* or the *ee* in *meet* (when it's stressed). You can find this sound in words like *inglés* (*English*), *argentino* (*Argentinian*) or *salir* (*to go out*).

Letter *o* always sounds like the *o* in *tongue*. You can find this sound in words like *tomate* (*tomato*) and *vaso* (*glass*).

Letter *u* always sounds like the *oo* in *pool* or like English *w* in *water*. You can find this sound in words like *luna* (*moon*) and *usar* (*to use*).

Consonants

Letter *b* in Spanish is similar to letter *b* in English, but while in English it sounds harder when it's in the beginning of a word (as in *beautiful*), in Spanish it's always a soft sound (as in *cabin*). You will find it in words like *bebé* (*baby*).

Letter *c* in Spanish can have three sounds:

The first is like the *c* in *cut*. Letter *c* always sounds like this when it comes before letters *a, o, u* and consonants (except *h*), as in words like *cama* (*bed*), *cosa* (*thing*), *cuento* (*tale*) and *acto*.

The second *c* sound is the same as the *s* sound. It sounds like this when it comes before letters *e* and *i*, as in *cerilla* (*match*) or *cien* (*a hundred*).

The third sound is only possible when *c* comes before an *h*, just as it happens in English. The combination of *c* and *h* sounds like *ch* in *change*. You will find this in words like *colchón* (*mattress*).

Letter **d** in Spanish is similar to *d* in English (as in *daisy*), but softer. You can find it in words such as *dedo* (*finger*).

Letter **f** in Spanish sounds like *f* in English, in words such as *fish*. You will find this sound in Spanish words like *feliz* (*happy*).

Letter **g** in Spanish can have two different sounds:

When it comes before letters *a, o, u* and consonants it sounds like a soft version of the English *g* sound in *green*. You can find this sound in words like *gato* (cat), *gota* (*drop*), *gusto* (*taste*) and *gracias* (*thanks*). You also get this sound when you have the combination of letters *gue* and *gui*. In these cases, the *u* is not pronounced, just as it happens in English in *guest* or *guilty*. You can find this sound in Spanish in words such as *guerra* (*war*) and *guitarra* (*guitar*). The *u* is only pronounced when there's a dieresis (two dots) on top of it, as in *pingüino* (*penguin*) or *antigüedad* (*antique*), but this is not very common.

The second *g* sound in Spanish is similar to the *h* sound in English word *helicopter*. You can find this sound when *g* comes before letters *e* and *i*, as in *gente* (*people*) or *girasol* (*sunflower*).

Letter **h** in Spanish is mute. You will normally find it at the beginning of words, such as *hielo* (*ice*) or *huevo* (*egg*), but it can also be in the middle, as in *almohada* (*pillow*). The only situation where *h* has a sound is in combination with *c*, as in *chocolate* (*chocolate*).

Letter **j** in Spanish sounds like the Spanish *g* before letters *e* and *i*. This means it sounds similar to English *h* in words like *heaven*. You can find this letter in words such as *jamón* (*ham*), *jefe* (*boss*) and *joven* (*young*).

Letter **k** is not used in many words in Spanish, but you can find it in some, like *kilo* (*kilo*) and *kiosco* (*kiosk*). The sound is the same as the sound of letter *c* when it comes before letters *a, o, u* and consonants, as in *cantar* (*to sing*).

Letter **l** in Spanish sounds exactly as letter *l* in English. You can find it in words such as *limón* (*lemon*) or *loco* (*crazy*). However, when two *l* are put together, the sound changes. The combination *ll* sounds different in some Latin American countries and in Spain. In different regions it's pronounced like the Spanish *i* or *li* letters, like the English *y* in <u>y</u>ellow or *j* in <u>j</u>ello or like the English *sh* in <u>sh</u>ow.

Letter *m* in Spanish always sounds like the *m* in English, as in <u>m</u>onster. You can find this letter in words like <u>m</u>iedo (*fear*) or <u>m</u>ejor (*better*).

Letter *n* in Spanish always sounds like the *n* in English, as in <u>n</u>o<u>n</u>sense. You can find this letter in words like <u>n</u>u<u>n</u>ca (*never*) or <u>n</u>ada (*nothing*).

Letter *ñ* sounds like the combination of letters *ni*, as in *nibble*. You can find this letter in words as ni<u>ñ</u>o (*kid*), where the *ni* and the *ñ* sound exactly the same. Other words with letter *ñ* are contrase<u>ñ</u>a (*password*), se<u>ñ</u>al (*signal*) and due<u>ñ</u>o (*owner*).

Letter *p* in Spanish sounds softer than the English *p*. It is actually more similar to the English *b* in <u>b</u>ecause. You can find this sound in words like <u>p</u>erro (*dog*) or rá<u>p</u>ido (*fast*).

Letter *q* is only used in Spanish in the combinations *que* and *qui*. In these cases, the *u* is silent and the *q* sounds like *c* when it comes before letters *a, o, u* and consonants, as in <u>c</u>o<u>c</u>o (*coconut*). You can find letter *q* in words like <u>q</u>ueso (*cheese*) and <u>q</u>uizás (*maybe*).

Letter *r* has two different sounds in Spanish:

> The strong *r* sound is very difficult to non-Spanish speakers, so if you want to roll your *r* like a local you need to try to place your tongue in the front of your palate, right behind your teeth, and try to make air pass through until it sounds like a starting engine. You'll need this sound for words that start with *r*, like <u>r</u>ata (*rat*), and for words that have a double *r*, like pe<u>rr</u>o (*dog*).

> The soft *r* is easier, and it sounds like the American sound for *t* in wa<u>t</u>er. You'll use the soft *r* in words like ca<u>r</u>a (*face*).

Letter *s* always sounds like the *s* in <u>s</u>nake. You'll use this sound in words like <u>s</u>illa (*chair*) or <u>S</u>ol (*sun*).

Letter *t* sounds stronger than American *t* and a little bit softer than British *t*. You'll use this sound in words like <u>t</u>oma<u>t</u>e (*tomato*) and <u>t</u>echo (*roof*).

Letter *v* sounds similar to English *v*, maybe a little bit softer and sometimes not really different to *b*. You'll find this sound in words like <u>v</u>aca (*cow*) and <u>v</u>aso (*glass*).

Letter *w* is not really common in Spanish. It is only used in word with a foreign origin, like those who come from English. It is pronounced like the English *w* and you'll find it in words like ki<u>w</u>i and sho<u>w</u>, which mean the same as in English.

Letter *x* is also not a really common word in Spanish. It sounds like a strong *c* and an *s* put together, just like in English. You'll use it in words like ta<u>x</u>i (*taxi*) and cone<u>x</u>ión (*connection*).

Letter *y* has two different sounds:

It sounds like Spanish *i* (like the *i* in *intelligence* or the *ee* in *meet*) in words like *y* (*and*) or *hoy* (*today*).

It can sound like Spanish *ll* and also sounds different in some Latin American countries and in Spain: it's pronounced like the Spanish *i*, like the English *y* in *yellow* or *j* in *jello* or like the English *sh* in *show*. You'll find this in really common words like *yo* (*I*) and *ya* (*now*).

Letter *z* is pronounced, in some countries, like an *s*; but in some others it's quite different (for example, in Spain): it sounds similar to the *th* in *with* or *throne*. You'll use the *z* in words like *cazar* (*to hunt*) and *zorro* (*fox*) .

Chapter 2 - Standard phrases in Spanish

Here is a list of the most important standard phrases of the Spanish language. We will provide you with some everyday words as well as phrases you can use when you make small-talk with a stranger or a friend.

Basic phrases like "hello", "please", "thank you," and "goodbye" are very helpful at the beginning.

Everyday words

sí - yes

no - no

por favor - please

gracias - thank you

permiso - excuse me

¿disculpe? - pardon?

lo siento/perdón - I'm sorry

¿dónde? - where?

¿por qué? - why?

¿cuándo? - when?

¿quién? - who?

¿cómo? - how?

aquí - here

allí - there

Understanding

Comprendo - I understand

No comprendo - I don't understand

Por favor, hable más despacio - Please speak slowly

¿Podría repetir eso, por favor? - Could you repeat that, please?

¿Podría escribir eso, por favor? - Could you write that down, please?

¿Habla inglés? - Do you speak English?

¿Habla español? - Do you speak Spanish?

¿Habla francés? - Do you speak French?

¿Habla alemán? - Do you speak German?

¿Habla italiano? - Do you speak Italian?

Signs

abierto - open

cerrado - closed

entrada - entrance

salida - exit

empuje - push

tire - pull

hombres - men

mujeres - women

ocupado - occupied

libre - vacant

Greeting

¿Cómo estás/está? (informal/formal speech) - How are you?

Bien - Well

Bastante bien - Quite well

No tan bien - Not so good

Hola - Hello

Buenos días - Good morning

Buenas tardes - Good afternoon/evening

Buenas noches - Night

Chau - Bye

Adiós - Goodbye

¿Cómo te llamas? - What is your name?

Mi nombre es… - My name is…

¿De dónde eres? - Where are you from?

Yo soy de… - I'm from…

Hasta luego - See you later

Tenga un buen día - Have a nice day

¡Buen fin de semana! - Have a good weekend!

Cuídate - Take care

Igualmente - You too

Nos vemos - See you

To apologize/thank someone

Perdón - Sorry

Lo lamento - I am sorry

Gracias - Thanks

Muchas gracias - Thank you very much

De nada - You are welcome

No hay por qué - Never mind

Está bien - It's fine

Compliments

Eso se ve muy bien - That looks good

Eres muy amable - You are very nice

Te ves muy bien - You look really good

¡Buen trabajo! - Good job!

¡Bien hecho! - Well done!

How are you?

¿Cómo estás tú?/¿Cómo está usted? (informal/formal) - How are you/you?

Estoy bien - I'm fine

Bien, ¿y tú? – Good, and you?

No me estoy sintiendo bien - I am not feeling well

Asking for opinions and expressing yourself

¿Qué piensas? - What do you think?

Creo que… - I think that…

Espero que… - I hope that…

Me temo que… - I'm afraid that…

En mi opinión… - In my opinión…

Estoy de acuerdo - I agree

No estoy de acuerdo - I disagree

Es cierto - That's true

No es cierto - That's not true

Creo que sí - I think so

No lo creo - I don't think so

Espero que sí - I hope so

Espero que no - I hope not

Tienes razón - You're right

Estás equivocado - You're wrong

No me importa - I don't mind

Depende de ti - It's up to you

Eso depende - That depends

Eso es interesante - That's interesting

Eso es gracioso - That's funny

Traveling by public transport

¿Cuándo viene el próximo tren a la estación central? - When is the next train to the main station?

¿Qué pasaje necesito para ir hasta [parada]? - Which ticket/price level do I need until [stop]?

¿Desde qué andén parte este tren? - From which track is this train departing?

El tren tiene un retraso de 10 minutos - The train is 10 minutes late

¿Este asiento está libre? - Is this seat free?

Getting to know each other

¿Cómo te llamas? - What is your name?

Me llamo… - My name is…

¿De dónde eres? - Where are you from?

Soy de… - I'm from…

¿En qué trabajas? - What do you do for work?

Soy… - I am…

¿Desde cuándo estás en…? - Since when are you in…?

¿Conoces…? - Do you know…?

Make an appointment

¿Quieres ir al cine mañana? - Do you want to go to the cinema tomorrow?

Vayamos al cine mañana - Let's go to the cinema tomorrow

¿A qué hora quedamos? - When/At what time are we meeting?

¿Tienes tiempo mañana? - Do you have free time tomorrow?

Llámame… - Call me

Being upset with something/someone

¿Es una broma? - Is that supposed to be a joke?

¿Estás loco/a? - Are you crazy?

¡Debes estar loco/a! - You must have gone crazy!

¡Eso está muy mal! - That's very wrong!

Events and activities

¿Qué te interesa? - What are you interested in?

¿Hay algún/alguna… hoy? - Are there any… today?

exhibición - exhibition

evento cultural - cultural events

partido - sporting events

excursión - excursions

paseo - tours

¿Podría decirme qué hay en el/la…? - Could you tell me what's on at the…?

cine - cinema

teatro - theatre

sala de conciertos - concert hall

sala de ópera - opera house

¿Puedo reservar entradas aquí? - Can I book tickets here?

¿Tiene algún folleto sobre…? - Do you have any brochures on…?

atracciones locales - local attractions

¿Puede recomendar un buen restaurante? - Can you recommend a good restaurant?

¿Tiene un mapa de…? - Do you have a map of the…

la ciudad - city

el pueblo - town

¿Dónde está el…? - Where's the…?

centro de la ciudad - city centre

la galería de arte - art gallery

el museo - museum

la principal calle comercial - main shopping street

el mercado - market

la estación de trenes - railway station

¿Cuál es la mejor forma de moverse en la ciudad? - What's the best way of getting around the city?

¿Dónde puedo alquilar un auto? - Where can I rent a car?

Religion

¿Eres religioso? - Are you religious?

No, soy… - No, I'm…

Ateo - an atheist

Agnóstico - agnostic

¿A qué religión perteneces? - What religion are you?

Soy… - I'm a…

Cristiano - Christian

Protestante - Protestant

Católico - Catholic

Judío - Jewish

Musulmán - Muslim

Budista - Buddhist

Hindú - Hindu

¿Crees en Dios? - Do you believe in God?

Creo en Dios - I believe in God

No creo en Dios - I don't believe in God

¿Crees en la vida después de la muerte? - Do you believe in life after death?

¿Crees en la reencarnación? - Do you believe in reincarnation?

¿Hay un/una… cerca de aquí? - Is there a… nearby?

una iglesia - church

una mezquita - mosque

una sinagoga - synagogue

un templo - temple

Chapter 3 - Numbers and Colors

Numbers are everywhere and they are important because of many reasons. When you find yourself somewhere and need to know the time or if you need to tell someone how much something costs, then you will certainly find this helpful:

un/uno - one

dos - two

tres - three

cuatro - four

cinco - five

seis - six

siete - seven

ocho - eight

nueve - nine

diez - ten

once - eleven

doce - twelve

trece - thirteen

catorce - fourteen

quince - fifteen

dieciséis - sixteen

diecisiete - seventeen

dieciocho - eighteen

diecinueve - nineteen

veinte - twenty

veintiuno - twenty one

veintidós - twenty two

veintitrés - twenty three

treinta - thirty

cuarenta - forty

cincuenta - fifty

sesenta - sixty

setenta - seventy

ochenta - eighty

noventa - ninety

cien - one hundred

doscientos - two hundred

trescientos - three hundred

mil - one thousand

dos mil - two thousand

un millón - one million

medio - half

menos de - less than

más de - more than

Time

ahora - now

después - after

más tarde - later

antes - before

mañana - morning

tarde - afternoon

noche - evening

noche - night

hoy - today

ayer - yesterday

mañana - tomorrow

esta semana - this week

la semana pasada - last week

la próxima semana - next week

la una de la mañana - one o'clock AM

las dos de la mañana - two o'clock AM

el mediodía - noon

la una de la tarde - one o'clock PM

las dos de la tarde - two o'clock PM

la medianoche - midnight

ocho y media - half past eight

ocho y cuarto - quarter past eight

ocho menos cuarto - quarter to eight

minutos - minutes

horas - hours

días - days

semanas - weeks

meses - months

años - years

Days of the week

lunes - Monday

martes - Tuesday

miércoles - Wednesday

jueves - Thursday

viernes - Friday

sábado - Saturday

domingo - Sunday

Months

enero - January

febrero - February

marzo - March

abril - April

mayo - May

junio - June

julio - July

agosto - August

septiembre - September

octubre - October

noviembre - November

diciembre - December

Colours

negro - black

blanco - white

gris - grey

rojo - red

azul - blue

amarillo - yellow

verde - green

naranja - orange

violeta - purple

marrón – brown

Chapter 4 - Transport

The streets can be complicated sometimes and with all the cars, buses and trains, one gets lost easily. You will probably use public transport to move around, or you may go for a walk and need help reaching your destination.

Either way, you should remember a few simple questions to ask for directions, to buy tickets, or to find your way around. If you can tell people where you want to go, you should find your way with a little luck. Even if you do not understand otherwise, these phrases will help you direct your taxi drivers and get rudimentary advice from people on the street.

Here are some of the most important phrases to get you to your destination as soon as possible.

Bus and Train

¿Cuánto cuesta un pasaje/boleto/billete a…? - How much is a ticket to…?

Un pasaje a…, por favor - One ticket to…, please.

¿A dónde va este tren/bus? - Where does this train/bus go?

¿Dónde para el tren/bus a…? - Where does the train/bus to… stop?

¿Cuándo parte el tren/bus a…? - When does the train/bus for… leave?

¿Cuándo llega el tren/bus a…? - When will this train/bus arrive in…?

¿Dónde está la boletería? - Where's the ticket office?

¿Dónde están las máquinas de boletos? - Where are the ticket machines?

¿Cuándo parte el próximo bus a…? - What time's the next bus to…?

¿Cuál es el horario del próximo tren a…? - What time's the next train to…?

¿Puedo comprar el boleto en el bus? - Can I buy a ticket on the bus?

¿Puedo comprar el boleto en el tren? - Can I buy a ticket on the train?

¿Cuánto cuesta el boleto a…? - How much is a ticket to…?

de ida - single

ida y vuelta - return

primera clase - first class

un viaje de ida para un menor - child single

un viaje de ida y vuelta para un menor - child return

un viaje de ida para un mayor - senior citizens' single

un viaje de ida y vuelta para un mayor - Senior citizens' return

¿Hay algún descuento? - are there any reductions?

¿Cuándo le gustaría viajar? - When would you like to travel?

¿Cuándo volverá? - When will you be coming back?

Me gustaría volver a…… el domingo - I'd like a return to… on Sunday

¿A qué plataforma debo dirigirme para…? - Which platform do I need for…?

¿Es esta la plataforma para…? - Is this the right platform for…?

¿Dónde cambio para…? - Where do I change for…?

Necesita cambiar en… - You'll need to change at…

¿Tiene un horario, por favor? - Can I have a timetable, please?

¿Cuál es la frecuencia de los buses a…? - How often do the buses run to…?

¿Cuál es la frecuencia de los trenes a…? - How often do the trains run to…?

Me gustaría renovar mi pase dc temporada, por favor - I'd like to renew my season ticket, please

El tren tiene un retraso - The train's running late

El tren se canceló - The train's been cancelled

¿Se detiene este bus en…? - Does this bus stop at…?

¿Se detiene este tren en…? - Does this train stop at…?

¿Puedo poner esto en el portaequipaje, por favor? - Could I put this in the hold, please?

¿Podría decirme cuándo llegaremos a…? - Could you tell me when we get to…?

¿Podría por favor detenerse en…? - Could you please stop at…?

¿Le molesta si me siento aquí? - Do you mind if I sit here?

Billetes, por favor - Tickets, please

Todos los boletos y tarjetas, por favor - All tickets and railcards, please

¿Podría ver su pasaje, por favor? - Could I see your ticket, please?

Perdí mi billete - I've lost my ticket

¿A qué hora llegamos a…? - What time do we arrive in…?

¿Cuál es esta parada? - What's this stop?

¿Cuál es la próxima parada? - What's the next stop?

Esta es mi parada - This is my stop

Debo bajar aquí - I'm getting off here

¿Hay un restaurante en el tren? - Is there a buffet car on the train?

¿Le molesta si abro la ventanilla? - Do you mind if I open the window?

Este tren finaliza aquí - This train terminates here

Todos los pasajeros deben bajarse, por favor - All passengers must get down, please

Por favor, lleve todo su equipaje y bienes personales con usted - Please take all your luggage and personal belongings with you

¿Cuántas paradas/estaciones faltan para…? - How many stops is it to…?

Me gustaría un pase diario, por favor - I'd like a Day Travelcard, please

¿Para qué zonas? - Which zones?

Direction

¿Cómo llego a…? - How do I get to…?

…la estación central de trenes? - …the train station?

…la estación central de buses? - …the bus station?

…el aeropuerto? - …the airport?

…el centro? - …downtown?

…el hostal? - …the hostel?

…el hotel? - …the hotel?

…el consulado? - …the consulate?

¿Dónde puedo encontrar…? - Where are there…

…hoteles? - …hotels?

…restaurantes? - …restaurants?

…bares? - …bars?

…buenas vistas? - …sights to see?

¿Me lo puede mostrar en el mapa? - Can you show me on the map?

calle - street

Gire a la izquierda - Turn left.

Gire a la derecha - Turn right.

izquierda - left

derecha - right

recto - straight ahead

hacia el/la… - towards the…

después del/de la… - past the…

antes del/de la… - before the…

Norte - north

Sur - south

Este - east

Oeste - west

en subida - uphill

en bajada - downhill

Taxi

¡Taxi! - Taxi!

Lléveme a…, por favor - Take me to…, please

¿Cuánto cuesta ir hasta…? - How much does it cost to get to…?

Lléveme allí, por favor - Take me there, please.

¿Cómo de largo es el viaje? - How long will the journey take?

¿Le molesta si abro la ventana? - Do you mind if I open the window?

¿Le molesta si cierro la ventana? - Do you mind if I close the window?

¿Ya estamos cerca? - Are we almost there?

¿Cuánto es? - How much is it?

Guarde el cambio - That's fine, keep the change

¿Le gustaría un recibo? - Would you like a receipt?

¿Me podría dar el recibo, por favor? - Could I have a receipt, please?

¿Podría pasarme a buscar a las…? - Could you pick me up here at… (time)?

¿Podría esperarme aquí? - Could you wait for me here?

¿Dónde está? - Where are you?

¿Cuál es la dirección? - What's the address?

Estoy en… - I'm at…

el hotel - the hotel

la estación central - the train station

¿Cuál es su nombre? - Could I take your name, please?

¿Cuánto tengo que esperar? - How long will I have to wait?

¿Cuánto tiempo tardará? - How long will it be?

Está en camino - It's on its way

¿A dónde le gustaría ir? - Where would you like to go?

Me gustaría ir a… - I'd like to go to…

A la estación central - to the train station

¿Podría llevarme a…? - Could you take me to…?

el centro de la ciudad - the city centre

¿Cuánto cuesta ir hasta…? - How much would it cost to…?

el aeropuerto - the airport

¿Podemos detenernos en un cajero automático? - Could we stop at a cashpoint?

¿El taxímetro está funcionando? - Is the meter switched on?

Por favor, inicie el taxímetro – Please, switch the meter on

Boat

¿Cuándo parte el próximo barco a…? - What time's the next boat to…?

Me gustaría un camarote con… - I'd like a… cabin

dos camas - two - berth

cuatro camas - four - berth

No necesitamos un camarote - We don't need a cabin

Me gustaría un billete para un auto y dos pasajeros - I'd like a ticket for a car and two passengers

Me gustaría un pasaje para un pasajero a pie - I'd like a ticket for a foot passenger

¿Cuánto tarda el viaje? - How long does the crossing take?

¿A qué hora llega el ferry a…? - What time does the ferry arrive in…?

¿Cuánto tiempo antes de la partida debemos llegar? - How soon before the departure time do we have to arrive?

¿Dónde está la oficina de información? - Where's the information desk?

¿Dónde está el camarote número…? - Where's cabin number…?

¿En dónde se encuentra el/la…? - Where is the…?

el autoservicio - buffet

el restaurante - restaurant

el bar - bar

la tienda - shop

el cine - cinema

me siento mareado - I feel seasick

El mar está muy revuelto - The sea's very rough

El mar está bastante calmado - The sea's quite calm

Todos los pasajeros en automóvil, por favor diríjanse a sus automóviles para el desembarco - All car passengers, please make your way down to the car decks for disembarkation

Llegaremos a puerto en aproximadamente treinta minutos - We will be arriving in port in approximately 30 minutes' time

Por favor, liberen sus camarotes – Please, vacate your cabins

Important terms

horario - timetable

de ida - single

ida y vuelta - return

plataforma - platform

sala de espera - waiting room

boletería - ticket office

asiento - seat

número de asiento - seat number

portaequipaje - luggage rack

primera clase - first class

segunda clase - second class

inspector de billetes - ticket inspector

multa - penalty fare

restaurante - buffet car

vagón - carriage

compartimento - compartment

tren rápido - express train

guarda - guard

paso a nivel - level crossing

cierre de línea - line closure

tarjeta de viaje - railcard

vías - railway line

boleto de temporada - season ticket

señal - signal

tren cama - sleeper train

estación - station

estación de tren - railway station

barrera tarifaria - ticket barrier

andén - track

tren - train

conductor del tren - train driver

tarifa del tren - train fare

viaje en tren - train journey

tarjeta de viaje - travelcard

estación de metro/subterráneo - underground station

túnel - tunnel

conductor de autobus - bus driver

tarifa de bus - bus fare

viaje en bus - bus journey

parada de autobus - bus stop

carril para buses - bus lane

estación de buses - bus station

conductor - conductor

inspector - inspector

portaequipaje - luggage hold

la próxima parada - the next stop

bus nocturno - night bus

pedir la parada - request stop

ruta - route

estación terminal - terminus

Passport control and customs

¿Puedo ver su pasaporte, por favor? - Could I see your passport, please?

¿Desde dónde viaja? - Where have you travelled from?

¿Cuál es el motivo de su visita? - What's the purpose of your visit?

Estoy de vacaciones - I'm on holiday

Estoy en un viaje de negocios - I'm on business

Estoy visitando a familiares - I'm visiting relatives

¿Cuánto tiempo se quedará? - How long will you be staying?

¿Dónde se quedará? - Where will you be staying?

formulario de inmigración - immigration form

¡Disfrute su estancia! - Enjoy your stay!

¿Puede abrir su maleta, por favor? - Could you open your bag, please?

¿Tiene algo que declarar? - Do you have anything to declare?

Tiene que pagar impuestos por estos bienes - You have to pay duty on these items

Chapter 5 - Accommodation

When you arrive to your destination, you need to get into your accommodations. Do you want to book a room, ask for breakfast, or report to the front desk that you have lost your key? Do not worry! Learn only a few words and have the courage to use them, too, and you will be able to quickly understand! These simple phrases will help you out:

Finding accommodation

Estamos buscando alojamiento - We're looking for accommodation

Necesitamos un lugar donde dormir - We need somewhere to stay

¿Tiene una lista de…? - Do you have a list of…?

hoteles - hotels

bed and breakfasts - bed and breakfasts

hostales - hostels

campamentos - campsites

¿Qué tipo de alojamiento está buscando? - What sort of accommodation are you looking for?

¿Puede reservar alojamiento para mí? - Can you book accommodation for me?

Reservation

¿Puedo ver su pasaporte? - Could I see your passport?

¿Puede completar este formulario? - Could you please fill in this registration form?

¿Tiene habitaciones disponibles? - Do you have any rooms available?

¿Cuánto cuesta un cuarto para una persona/dos personas? - How much is a room for one person/two people?

¿El cuarto cuenta con… - Does the room come with…

…un baño? - …a bathroom?

…un teléfono? - …a telephone?

…una TV? - …a TV?

¿Puedo ver la habitación antes? - May I see the room first?

¿Tiene algo menos ruidoso? - Do you have anything quieter?

…más pequeño? - …smaller?

…más grande? - …bigger?

…más limpio? - …cleaner?

…más barato? - …cheaper?

OK, ¡me lo quedo! - OK, I'll take it

Me quedaré… noche/s - I will stay for… night/s

¿Puede sugerirme otro hotel? - Can you suggest another hotel?

¿Tiene caja fuerte? - Do you have a safe?

…armarios? -…lockers?

¿El desayuno/La cena está incluido/a? - Is breakfast/supper included?

¿A qué hora es el desayuno/la cena? - What time is breakfast/supper?

¿Podría tomar el desayuno en mi habitación, por favor? - Could I have breakfast in my room, please?

¿A qué hora cierra el bar? - What time does the bar close?

¿Podría ayudarlo con su equipaje? - Would you like any help with your luggage?

Por favor, ¿podría limpiar mi habitación? - Could you please clean my room?

¿Podría despertarme a las…? - Can you wake me at…?

Quiero hacer el check out - I want to check out

¿Dónde están los ascensores? - Where are the elevators?

Creo que hay un error en la cuenta - I think there's a mistake in this bill

¿Cómo le gustaría pagar? - How would you like to pay?

Pagaré… - I'll pay…

con tarjeta de crédito - by credit card

en efectivo - in cash

¿Ha usado el minibar? - Have you used the minibar?

No hemos usado el minibar - We haven't used the minibar

¿Puede alguien ayudarnos a bajar nuestro equipaje? - Could we have some help bringing our luggage down?

¿Tiene sitio para que guardemos nuestro equipaje? - Do you have anywhere we could leave our luggage?

¿Puede darme un recibo, por favor? - Could I have a receipt, please?

¿Puede llamar a un taxi, por favor? - Could you please call me a taxi?

Espero que haya pasado una agradable estadía/estancia - I hope you had an enjoyable stay

Realmente disfruté mi estadía/estancia - I've really enjoyed my stay

Realmente disfrutamos nuestra estadía/estancia - We've really enjoyed our stay

Camping

campamento - campsite

tienda - tent

caravana - caravan

autocaravana - motorhome

¿Tiene parcelas libres? - Do you have any free pitches?

¿Puedo aparcar junto a la parcela? - Can I park beside the pitch?

parcela con servicios - serviced pitch

parcela sin servicios - unserviced pitch

conexión eléctrica - electrical connection

¿Cuál es el precio por noche? - What is the charge per night?

¿Dónde están las duchas? - Where are the showers?

¿Dónde está la lavandería? - Where are the laundry facilities?

¿Esta es agua potable? - Is this drinking water?

¿Puedo pedirle una garrafa? - Can I borrow a gas cylinder?

Complaints

Me gustaría otra habitación - I would like a different room

No funciona la calefacción - The heating does not work

El aire acondicionado no funciona - The air conditioning does not work

La habitación es muy ruidosa - The room is very noisy

La habitación huele mal - The room smells bad

Pedí una habitación para no fumadores - I requested a non - smoking room

Pedí una habitación con vista - I requested a room with a view

Mi llave no funciona - My key does not work

La ventana no abre - The window does not open

La habitación no ha sido limpiada - The room has not been cleaned

Hay ratones/ratas/insectos en la habitación - There are mice/rats/bugs in the room

No hay agua caliente - There is no hot water

No recibí mi llamada de despertador - I did not receive my wake - up call

Hay gastos de más en mi cuenta - The bill is overcharged

Mi vecino hace demasiado ruido - My neighbour is too loud

Important terms

entrada - check-in

salida - check-out

reserva - reservation

habitación disponible - vacant room

reservar - to book

registrarse - to check in

salir/hacer checkout - to check out

pagar la cuenta - to pay the bill

quedarse en un hotel - to stay at a hotel

hotel - hotel

bread and breakfast - B&B

casa de huéspedes - guesthouse

hostal - hostel

campamento - campsite

habitación simple - single room

habitación doble - double room

habitación doble con camas separadas - twin room

habitación con tres camas - triple room

suite - suite

aire acondicionado - air conditioning

baño - toilet

baño en suite - en - suite bathroom

acceso a internet - internet access

minibar - minibar

caja fuerte - safe

ducha - shower

bar - bar

estacionamiento/aparcamiento - parking lot

pasillo/corredor - corridor

salida de incendio - fire escape

habitación de juegos - games room

gimnasio - gym

servicio de lavandería - laundry service

ascensor - lift

vestíbulo - lobby

recepción - reception

restaurante - restaurant

servicio de habitaciones - room service

sauna - sauna

piscina - swimming pool

encargado/a - manager

empleado/a de limpieza - housekeeper

recepcionista - receptionist

portero - doorman

alarma de incendios - fire alarm

lavandería - laundry

llave de la habitación - room key

número de la habitación - room number

llamada de despertador - wake-up call

Chapter 6 - Money

When you visit another country and have to deal with different currencies, it's very useful to know how to ask someone for help or for the price of something.

¿Acepta dólares americanos? - Do you accept American dollars?

¿Acepta libras esterlinas? - Do you accept British pounds?

¿Acepta euros? - Do you accept Euros?

¿Acepta tarjeta de crédito? - Do you accept credit cards?

¿Puede cambiar dinero para mí? - Can you change money for me?

¿Dónde puedo cambiar dinero? - Where can I get money changed?

¿Puede cambiar un cheque de viajero para mí? - Can you change a traveler's check for me?

¿Dónde puedo cambiar un cheque de viajero? - Where can I get a traveler's check changed?

¿Cuál es la tasa de cambio? - What is the exchange rate?

¿Dónde hay un cajero automático? - Where is an ATM?

Chapter 7 - Restaurants and Food

Tasting different foods and trying the local cuisine is certainly one of the best parts of visiting a foreign country. Before you sit down at a local restaurant before a big meal, you should of course take some time to find out how to talk to the waiter or waitress or how to order your dish. Many restaurants offer menus with translation, but if you also want to move beyond the tourist trails, you may have to come to terms with a menu in Spanish! Our list with some basic words and sentences will help you:

Reservation and ordering

Una mesa para uno/dos, por favor - A table for one person/two people, please

¿Puedo ver el menú, por favor? - Can I look at the menu, please?

¿Puedo ver la cocina? - Can I look in the kitchen?

¿Hay una especialidad de la casa? - Is there a house specialty?

¿Hay una especialidad local? - Is there a local specialty?

Soy vegetariano/a - I'm a vegetarian

No como cerdo - I don't eat pork

No como carne de vaca - I don't eat beef

Solo como comida kosher - I only eat kosher food

a la carta - a la carte

desayuno - breakfast

almuerzo - lunch

merienda - tea - time

cena - dinner

Me gustaría… - I would like…

Quiero un plato que tenga… - I want a dish containing…

pollo - chicken

ternera - beef

pescado - fish

jamón - ham

salchichas - sausages

queso - cheese

huevos - eggs

ensalada - salad

verduras - vegetables

fruta - fruit

pan - bread

tostadas - toast

fideos - noodles

pasta - pasta

arroz - rice

frijoles - beans

patatas - potatoes

¿Puedo tomar un vaso de…? - May I have a glass of…?

¿Puedo tomar una copa de…? - May I have a cup of…?

¿Puedo tomar una botella de…? - May I have a bottle of…?

café - coffee

té - tea

jugo/zumo - juice

agua - water

cerveza - beer

vino tinto/blanco - red/white wine

¿Podría traerme...? - May I have some...?

sal - salt

pimienta - black pepper

manteca - butter

¿Disculpe, mesero/camarero/mozo? - Excuse me, waiter?

He terminado - I'm finished

Estaba delicioso - It was delicious

Por favor, llévese los platos - Please clear the plates

La cuenta, por favor - The check, please

Ordering snacks

¿Tiene bocadillos? - Do you have any snacks?

¿Tiene sándwiches? - Do you have any sandwiches?

¿Sirven comida? - Do you serve food?

¿A qué hora cierra la cocina? - What time does the kitchen close?

¿Aún se sirve comida aquí? - Are you still serving food?

Unas patatas fritas de bolsa, por favor - A packet of crisps, please

¿Qué sabor le gustaría? - What flavour would you like?

saladas - salted

queso y cebolla - Cheese and onion

sal y vinagre - Salt and vinegar

¿Qué tipo de sándwiches tienen? - What sort of sandwiches do you have?

¿Tienen platos calientes? - Do you have any hot food?

Los especiales del día están en la pizarra - Today's specials are on the board

¿Es servicio a la carta o autoservicio? - Is it table service or self - service?

¿Qué le puedo traer? - What can I get you?

¿Quiere algo de comer? - Would you like anything to eat?

¿Podemos ver un menú, por favor? - Could we see a menu, please?

¿Para llevar o para comer aquí? - Eat in or take - away?

Important terms

fresco - fresh

viejo - mouldy

podrido - rotten

jugoso - juicy

maduro - ripe

verde - unripe

tierno - tender

duro - tough

quemado - burnt

pasado - over - cooked

crudo - under - done/raw

bien cocido - well done

delicioso - delicious

horrible - horrible

salado - salty

salado - savoury

dulce - sweet

agrio - sour

sabroso - tasty

picante - spicy/hot

suave - mild

hornear - to bake

hervir - to boil

freír - to fry

asar a la parrilla - to grill

asar - to roast

cocer al vapor - to steam

desayuno - breakfast

almuerzo - lunch

merienda - tea - time

cena - dinner

desayunar - to have breakfast

almorzar - to have lunch

cenar - to have dinner

ingrediente - ingredient

receta - recipe

cocinar - to cook

poner la mesa - to set the table

levantar/recoger la mesa - to clear the table

sentarse a la mesa - to come to the table

limpiar la mesa - to wipe the table

preparar una comida - to prepare a meal

el bar - the bar

cocinero/chef - cook/chef

reserva - reservation

menú - menu

mesero/camarero/mozo - waiter

mesera/camarera/moza - waitress

carta de vinos - wine list

entrante/entrada/aperitivo - starter

plato principal - main course

postre - dessert

servicio - service

cobro de servicio - service charge

propina - tip

Chapter 8 - Bars

You can easily order your favorite drinks in a bar if you use these phrases below!

Ordering drinks

¿Se sirve alcohol? - Do you serve alcohol?

¿Hay servicio de mesa? - Is there table service?

Una cerveza/dos cervezas, por favor - A beer/two beers, please

Un vaso de vino tinto/blanco, por favor - A glass of red/white wine, please

Un vaso, por favor - A glass, please

Una pinta, por favor - A pint, please

Una botella, por favor - A bottle, please

whisky - whisky

vodka - vodka

ron - rum

agua - water

soda - soda

agua tónica - tonic water

jugo/zumo de naranja - orange juice

¿Tiene bocadillos? - Do you have any bar snacks?

Uno más, por favor - One more, please

Otra ronda, por favor - Another round, please

¿Cuándo cierra el bar? - When is closing time?

¿Qué le gustaría beber? - What would you like to drink?

¿Qué va a pedir? - What are you having?

¿Qué le puedo traer? - What can I get you?

Voy a querer…, por favor - I'll have…, please

una pinta de cerveza - a pint of lager

una copa de vino blanco - a glass of white wine

una copa de vino tinto - a glass of red wine

un zumo de naranja - an orange juice

un café - a coffee

una cola/una Coca Cola - a Coke

una Coca Cola Light - a Diet Coke

¿Grande o pequeño/a? - Large or small?

¿Lo quiere con hielo? - Would you like ice with that?

Sin hielo, por favor - No ice, please

Un poco, por favor - A little, please

Mucho hielo, por favor - Lots of ice, please

Una cerveza, por favor - A beer, please

Dos cervezas, por favor - Two beers, please

Tres chupitos de tequila, por favor - Three shots of tequila, please

¿Ya está atendido? - Are you already being served?

Estamos atendidos, gracias - We're being served, thanks

¿Quién sigue? - Who's next?

¿Qué vino le gustaría? - Which wine would you like?

El vino de la casa está bien - House wine is fine

¿Qué cerveza le gustaría? - Which beer would you like?

¿Le gustaría cerveza tirada o en botella? - Would you like draught or bottled beer?

Lo mismo para mí, por favor - I'll have the same, please

Nada para mí, gracias - Nothing for me, thanks

Quiero esto - I'll get this

¡Quédese con el cambio! - Keep the change!

¡Salud! - Cheers!

¿A quién le toca pagar la ronda? - Whose round is it?

Me toca pagar la ronda - It's my round

Te toca pagar la ronda - It's your round

Otra cerveza, por favor - Another beer, please

Dos cervezas más, por favor - Another two beers, please

Lo mismo otra vez, por favor - Same again, please

¿Aún sirven bebidas? - Are you still serving drinks?

¡Última ronda! - Last orders!

Asking for internet and WiFi

¿Tiene internet aquí? - Do you have internet access here?

¿Tiene wifi aquí? - Do you have WiFi here?

¿Cuál es la contraseña para usar internet? - What's the password for the internet?

The day after

Me siento bien - I feel fine

Me siento terrible - I feel terrible

Tengo resaca - I've got a hangover

¡Nunca beberé de nuevo! - I'm never going to drink again!

Smoking

¿Fumas? - Do you smoke?

No, no fumo - No, I don't smoke

Lo he dejado - I've given up

¿Te molesta si fumo? - Do you mind if I smoke?

¿Quieres un cigarrillo? - Would you like a cigarette?

¿Tienes un mechero? - Have you got a lighter?

Important terms

jugo/zumo de frutas - fruit juice

jugo/zumo de naranja - orange juice

té helado - iced tea

limonada - lemonade

batido - milkshake

agua - water

agua mineral - mineral water

agua con gas - sparkling water

agua del grifo - tap water

chocolatada - cocoa

café - coffee

café negro - black coffee

café descafeinado - decaffeinated coffee

té verde - green tea

té de hierbas - herbal tea

chocolate caliente - hot chocolate

té - tea

saquito de té - tea bag

fuerte - strong

cerveza - beer

vino - wine

vino tinto - red wine

vino blanco - white wine

vino rosado - rosé

vino espumoso - sparkling wine

champaña - champagne

licor - liqueur

ron - rum

whisky - whisky

vodka - vodka

alcohol - alcohol

bar - bar

tabernero/camarero/barman - barman

vaso de cerveza - beer glass

botella - bottle

lata - can

cóctel - cocktail

borracho/ebrio - drunk

resaca - hangover

sobrio - sober

bebidas alcohólicas/espirituosas - spirits

copa de vino - wine glass

Chapter 9 - Shopping

You want to buy a few souvenirs quickly? Or maybe you need to buy groceries? To make shopping quick and problem-free, we have the most important phrases here:

¿Tiene esto de mi talla? - Do you have this in my size?

¿Cuánto cuesta esto? - How much is this?

Es demasiado caro - That's too expensive

¿Aceptaría…? - Would you take…?

caro - expensive

barato - cheap

No me alcanza - I don't have enough

No lo quiero - I don't want it

Me está estafando - You're cheating me

No me interesa - I'm not interested

OK, me lo llevo - OK, I'll take it

¿Tiene una bolsa? - Can I have a bag?

¿Hace envíos? - Do you ship?

¿Tiene talles grandes? - Do you stock large sizes?

Necesito… - I need…

dentífrico - toothpaste

un cepillo de dientes - a toothbrush

tampones - tampons

jabón - soap

shampoo/champú - shampoo

analgésicos - pain reliever

medicina para el resfriado - cold medicine

medicina para el estómago - stomach medicine

una afeitadora - a razor

un paraguas - an umbrella

protector/loción solar - sun lotion

una postal - a postcard

estampillas - stamps

un cargador de teléfono - a phone charger

un adaptador - a power adaptor

baterías - batteries

un bolígrafo - a pen

Making a decision

Le queda bien - It suits you

Le quedan bien - They suit you

¿Lo tiene en otros colores? - Do you have it in different colours?

Me gustan - I like them

No me gustan - I don't like them

No me gusta el color - I don't like the colour

¿De qué están hechos? - What are these made of?

¿Pueden lavarse? - Are these washable?

No, deben ser lavados en seco - No, they have to be dry - cleaned

Me lo llevo - I'll take it

Me los llevo - I'll take them

Me llevo este - I'll take this one

Me llevo estos - I'll take these

Finding products

¿Podría decirme dónde está el/la…? - Could you tell me where the… is?

la leche - milk

la panadería - bread counter

la sección de carnes - meat section

la sección de congelados - frozen food section

¿Está atendido/a? - Are you being served?

Me gustaría… - I'd like…

ese trozo de queso - that piece of cheese

una porción de pizza - a slice of pizza

seis rodajas de jamón - six slices of ham

aceitunas - some olives

¿Cuánto le gustaría? - How much would you like?

300 gramos - 300 grams

medio kilo - half a kilo

Son $3.247 (tres mil doscientos cuarenta y siete pesos) - that's $3247

At a hair salon

Me gustaría un corte de cabello, por favor - I'd like a haircut, please

¿Es necesario hacer una reserva? - Do I need to book?

¿Está disponible ahora? - Are you able to see me now?

¿Quiere que le lave el cabello? - Would you like me to wash your hair?

¿Qué le gustaría? - What would you like?

¿Cómo quiere que se lo corte? - How would you like me to cut it?

Como usted quiera - However you want

Me gustaría… - I'd like…

un recorte - a trim

un nuevo estilo - a new style

una permanente - a perm

un flequillo - a fringe

reflejos/mechas - some highlights

un tinte - it coloured

¿Cómo de corto lo desea? - How short would you like it?

no demasiado corto - not too short

bastante corto - quite short

muy corto - very short

nivel uno - grade one

nivel dos - grade two

nivel tres - grade three

nivel cuatro - grade four

completamente rasurado - completely shaven

Así está bien, gracias - That's fine, thanks

¿Qué color le gustaría? - What colour would you like?

¿Cuál de estos colores desea? - Which of these colours would you like?

¿Podría recortar mi barba, por favor? - Could you trim my beard, please?

¿Cuánto es? - How much is it?

Important terms

barato - cheap

cliente - customer

descuento - discount

caro - expensive

precio - price

rebajas - sale

tienda - shop

bolsa de compras - shopping bag

lista de compras - shopping list

oferta especial - special offer

comprar - to buy

vender - to sell

pedir - to order

ir de compras - to go shopping

pasillo - aisle

cesta - basket

caja - counter

probador - fitting room

encargado - manager

estante - shelf

asistente de compras - shop assistant

vidriera - shop window

carrito - trolley

cajero - cashier

efectivo - cash

cambio - change

caja - checkout

queja - complaint

tarjeta de crédito - credit card

agotado - out of stock

bolsa de plástico - plastic bag

bolso/cartera - purse

fila/cola - queue

recibo - receipt

devolución/reintegro - refund

caja - till

cartera/billetera - wallet

Chapter 10 - Driving

If you plan on driving with your own car or renting one, then you should definitely know some rules and how to get to your destination without any issues. Have in mind that in Latin America and Spain gear sticks are quite common; in some countries, you might even have a hard time finding an automatic transmission. Here are some important phrases:

¿Puedo alquilar un automóvil? - Can I rent a car?

¿Tiene seguro? - Is it insuranced?

pare - stop

un sentido - one way

ceda el paso - yield

no estacionar/prohibido estacionar - no parking

límite de velocidad - speed limit

estación de servicio/gasolinera - gas station

gasolina/combustible/nafta - petrol/gas

diesel - diesel

Important terms

auto/coche/automóvil - car

caja de cambios - gear stick

transmisión automática - automatic transmission

calle principal - main road

autopista - highway

calle de un solo sentido - one - way street

carretera - road

esquina - corner

cruce - crossroads/junction

bifurcación - fork

paso a nivel - level crossing

acera - pavement/sidewalk

paso peatonal - pedestrian crossing

señal de tránsito - road sign

arcén - roadside

rotonda - roundabout

servicios - services

letrero - signpost

límite de velocidad - speed limit

semáforo - traffic light

giro - turn

accidente - accident

neumático pinchado - flat tyre

niebla - fog

multa por exceso de velocidad - speeding fine

atasco - traffic jam

chocar - to crash

choque - crash

tener un accidente - to have an accident

professor de autoescuela - driving instructor

clase de conducir - driving lesson

licencia de conducir - driving licence

autoescuela - driving school

examen de conducir - driving test

estacionamiento/aparcamiento - car park

aparcar/estacionar - to park

parquímetro - parking meter

multa - ticket

lavadero - car wash

diesel - diesel

aceite - oil

bicicleta - bike

bus - bus

caravana - caravan

motocicleta/moto - motorbike

taxi - taxi

camión - truck

coche de alquiler - rented car

llaves del coche - car keys

ciclista - cyclist

conductor - driver

garaje - garage

mecánico - mechanic

seguro - insurance

pasajero - passenger

peatón - pedestrian

marcha atrás - reverse gear

mapa - road map

GPS (ge pe ese) - GPS

velocidad - speed

tráfico - traffic

vehículo - vehicle

acelerar - to accelerate

frenar - to brake

conducir - to drive

bajar la velocidad - to slow down

aumentar la velocidad - to speed up

acelerador - accelerator

pedal de freno - brake pedal

freno de mano - handbrake

volante - steering wheel

batería - battery

motor - engine

tubo de escape - exhaust pipe

limpiaparabrisas - windscreen wiper

aire acondicionado - air conditioning

cierre centralizado - central locking

luces de freno - brake lights

espejo retrovisor - rear view mirror

asiento trasero - back seat

asiento para niños - child seat

asiento delantero - front seat

tanque de combustible - fuel tank

matrícula/placa - plate

número de matrícula/placa - plate number

cinturón de seguridad - seat belt

rueda de auxilio - spare wheel

ventana - window

parabrisas - windscreen

Chapter 11 - Authorities

If you have to deal with authorities, it's good to know some of the phrases to explain yourself and get out of a difficult situation. We hope you never have to use these!

No he hecho nada malo - I haven't done anything wrong

Fue un malentendido - It was a misunderstanding

¿A dónde me está llevando? - Where are you taking me?

¿Estoy bajo arresto? - Am I under arrest?

Soy un ciudadano… - I am a… citizen

Necesito comunicarme con el consulado/la embajada… - I need to talk to the… embassy/consulate

Quiero hablar con mi abogado - I want to talk to a lawyer

¿No puedo simplemente pagar una multa? - Can't I just pay a fine?

Necesito alguien que pueda traducir - I need someone who can translate for me

Chapter 12 - Emergencies and health

In case of an emergency, make sure to use these phrases. We also recommend that you know beforehand important local phone numbers, such as those to call the police, firefighters and ambulances.

Regarding health issues, make sure you have insurance and you have with yourself information in Spanish written down about serious allergies or health conditions. Before travelling, make sure you get all shots recommended by the WHO for the specific place you're visiting.

¡Ayuda! - Help!

¡Fuego! - Fire!

¡Sal de ahí! - Go away!

Llamaré a la policía - I'll call the police

¡Es urgente! - It's urgent!

Estoy perdido - I'm lost

He perdido… - I've lost…

mi pasaporte - my passport

las llaves de mi automóvil - my car keys

Me han robado - I've been robbed

He tenido un accidente - I've had an accident

Se ha roto mi coche - My car has broken down

Mi coche ha sido robado - My car has been stolen

Necesito… - I need…

combustible - petrol

un mecánico - a mechanic

a la policía - the police

Health

Necesito… - I need…

un doctor - a doctor

un teléfono - a telephone

una ambulancia - an ambulance

un intérprete - an interpreter

un dentista - a dentist

¿Dónde está el hospital? - Where is the hospital?

Soy alérgico/a a la penicilina - I'm allergic to penicillin

Soy… - I'm…

diabético/a - diabetic

asmático/a - asthmatic

Me duele aquí - It hurts here

Creo que está roto - I think it's broken

At the pharmacy

Necesito… - I need…

dentífrico - toothpaste

paracetamol - paracetamol

Tengo una receta de mi médico - I've got a prescription here from the doctor

¿Tiene algo para…? - have you got anything for…?

el dolor de garganta - a sore throat

la tos - a cough

el pie de atleta - athlete's foot

¿Puede recomendar algo para un resfriado? - Can you recommend anything for a cold?

Tengo… - I'm suffering from…

alergia al polen - hay fever

indigestión - indigestion

diarrea - diarrhoea

un sarpullido - I've got a rash

Puede probar esta crema - You could try this cream

Si no se le pasa en una semana, debería ver a un médico - If it doesn't clear up after a week, you should see your doctor

¿Puedo comprar esto sin receta? - Can I buy this without a prescription?

Solo está disponible con receta - It's only available on prescription

¿Tiene efectos secundarios? - Does it have any side - effects?

Debe evitar el alcohol - You should avoid alcohol

Visiting a doctor

Necesito ver a un médico - I'd like to see a doctor

¿Tiene cita? - Do you have an appointment?

¿Es urgente? - Is it urgent?

Me gustaría pedir una cita para ver al/a la Dr…. - I'd like to make an appointment to see Dr…

¿Hay doctores que hablen…? - Are there any doctors who speak…?

¿Tiene seguro médico? - Do you have private medical insurance?

Por favor, tome asiento – Please, take a seat

El doctor está listo para verlo/a - The doctor's ready to see you now

¿Cómo puedo ayudarlo/a? - How can I help you?

¿Cuál es el problema? - What's the problem?

¿Cuáles son los síntomas? - What are your symptoms?

Tengo… - I've got a…

fiebre - temperature

dolor de garganta - sore throat

dolor de cabeza - headache

un sarpullido - rash

Me siento enfermo/a - I've been feeling sick

Estoy muy congestionado/a - I'm very congested

Tengo diarrea - I've got diarrhea

Estoy estreñido/a - I'm constipated

Tengo un bulto - I've got a bump

Tengo un tobillo hinchado - I've got a swollen ankle

Me duele mucho - I'm in a lot of pain

Me duele… - I've got a pain in my…

la espalda - back

el pecho - chest

Necesito… - I need…

otro inhalador - another inhaler

más insulina - some more insulin

me cuesta respirar - I'm having difficulty breathing

Tengo poca energía - I've got very little energy

Me siento muy cansado - I've been feeling very tired

Me cuesta dormir - I've been having difficulty sleeping

¿Hace cuánto tiempo se siente así? - How long have you been feeling like this?

¿Puede ser que esté embarazada? - Is there any possibility you might be pregnant?

Creo que puedo estar embarazada - I think I might be pregnant

¿Tiene alergias? - Do you have any allergies?

Soy alérgico/a a los antibióticos - I'm allergic to antibiotics

¿Toma algún medicamento? - Are you on any sort of medication?

¿Dónde le duele? - Where does it hurt?

Me duele aquí - It hurts here

¿Duele cuando toco aquí? - Does it hurt when I press here?

Voy a tomar su… - I'm going to take your…

presión - blood pressure

temperatura - temperature

pulso - pulse

Su presión es… - Your blood pressure is…

bastante baja - quite low

normal - normal

bastante alta - rather high

muy alta - very high

Su temperatura es… - Your temperature's…

normal - normal

un poco alta - a little high

muy alta - very high

Abra su boca, por favor - Open your mouth, please

Tosa, por favor - Cough, please

Necesitará un par de puntos - You're going to need a few stitches

Le pondré una inyección - I'm going to give you an injection

Necesitamos… - We need…

una muestra de orina - urine sample

una muestra de sangre - blood sample

Necesitamos hacerle un análisis de sangre - You need to have a blood test

Le voy a recetar antibióticos - I'm going to prescribe you some antibiotics

Tome dos de estas píldoras/pastillas tres veces al día - Take two of these pills three times a day

¿Fuma? - Do you smoke?

Debe dejar de fumar - You should stop smoking

¿Cuánto alcohol bebe por semana? - How much alcohol do you drink a week?

Debería beber menos - You should cut down on your drinking

Necesita perder peso - You need to try and lose some weight

Important terms

antiséptico - antiseptic

aspirina - aspirin

talco - foot powder

vendas/banditas/curitas - bandages

jarabe para la tos - cough mixture

anticonceptivos de emergencia - emergency contraception

gotas para los ojos - eye drops

un equipo de primeros auxilios - first aid kit

laxantes - laxatives

medicina - medicine

analgésicos - painkillers

paracetamol - paracetamol

prueba de embarazo - pregnancy test

receta - prescription

pastillas para dormir - sleeping tablets

termómetro - thermometer

pañuelos - tissues

vitaminas - vitamins

preservativos/condones - condoms

pañales - diapers/nappies

termo - hot water bottle

protector/loción solar - sun cream

mejilla - cheek

mentón - chin

cabeza - head

cabello - hair

oreja/oído - ear

ojo - eye

ceja - eyebrow

pestaña - eyelash

párpado - eyelid

frente - forehead

mandíbula - jaw

labio - lip

boca - mouth

nariz - nose

lengua - tongue

diente - tooth

brazo - arm

axila - armpit

espalda - back

seno - breast

pecho - chest

codo - elbow

mano - hand

dedo - finger/toe

uña - fingernail/toenail

cucllo - neck

hombro - shoulder

garganta - throat

cintura - waist

muñeca - wrist

tobillo - ankle

ano - anus

vientre - belly

nalgas - buttocks

pie - foot

genitales - genitals

cadera - hip

rodilla - knee

pierna - leg

apéndice - appendix

vejiga - bladder

cerebro - brain

corazón - heart

intestinos - intestines

riñones - kidneys

hígado - liver

pulmones - lungs

esófago - oesophagus

órgano - organ

estómago - stomach

vena - vein

costilla - rib

esqueleto - skeleton

cráneo - skull

columna vertebral - spine

sangre - blood

flema - phlegm

saliva - saliva

sudor - sweat

lágrimas - tears

orina - urine

vómito - vomit

hueso - bone

articulación - joint

músculo - muscle

nervio - nerve

piel - skin

respirar - to breathe

llorar - to cry

estornudar - to sneeze

sudar - to sweat

orinar - to urinate

vomitar - to vomit

ver - to see

oír - to hear

oler - to smell

peine - comb

acondicionador/crema de enjuague - conditioner

hilo dental - dental floss

desodorante - deodorant

cepillo - hairbrush

enjuaguc bucal - mouthwash

alicate - nail scissors

perfume - perfume

navaja/máquina de afeitar/afeitadora - razor

toallas femeninas - sanitary towels

champú/shampoo - shampoo

jabón - soap

tampones - tampons

cepillo de dientes - toothbrush

dentífrico - toothpaste

pinzas - tweezers

algodón - cotton wool

delineador - eyeliner

sombra para ojos - eyeshadow

base - foundation

tinte para el cabello - hair dye

gel para el cabello - hair gel

crema de manos - hand cream

lapiz labial - lipstick

maquillaje - makeup

crema hidratante - moisturising cream

Chapter 13 - Services and repairs

If you have personal items that require repair or cleaning, these phrases will be helpful.

¿Sabe dónde puedo reparar mi…? - Do you know where I can get my… repaired?

¿Repara…? - Do you do… repairs?

teléfonos - phones

relojes - watches

cámaras - cameras

zapatos - shoes

ordenadores/computadoras/computadores - computer

La pantalla está rota - The screen is broken

¿Cuánto cuesta? - How much will it cost?

¿Cuándo estará listo? - When will it be ready?

¿Cuánto tardará? - How long will it take?

Lo puedo hacer ahora mismo - I can do it straight away

Estará listo… - It'll be ready…

mañana - by tomorrow

la semana próxima - next week

¿Puede repararlo? - Are you able to repair it?

No podemos hacerlo aquí - We can't do it here

No vale la pena repararlo - It's not worth repairing

Mi reloj dejó de funcionar - My watch has stopped

¿Puedo verlo? - Can I have a look at it?

Creo que necesita una batería nueva - I think it needs a new battery

Vengo a buscar mi… - I've come to collect my…

teléfono - phone

reloj - watch

computadora/ordenador/computador - computer

Bank

Me gustaría retirar €100 (cien euros), por favor - I'd like to withdraw €100, please

Quiero hacer un retiro de dinero - I want to make a withdrawal

¿Cómo le gustaría el dinero? - How would you like the money?

en billetes de diez, por favor - in tens, please

¿Podría darme billetes más chicos? - Could you give me some smaller notes?

Tiene…? - Have you got any…?

identificación - identification

Tengo… - I've got…

mi pasaporte – my passport

mi licencia de conducir – my driving licence

mi documento de identidad – my ID card

Su cuenta está sobregirada - Your account is overdrawn

Me gustaría transferir dinero a esta cuenta - I'd like to transfer some money to this account

Me gustaría abrir una cuenta - I'd like to open an account

¿Podría decirme mi saldo, por favor? - Could you tell me my balance, please?

Me gustaría cambiar dinero - I'd like to change some money

¿Cuál es la tasa de cambio para euros/dólares? - What's the exchange rate for euros/dollars?

Me gustaría cambiar… - I'd like to change some…

euros - euros

dólares estadounidenses - US dollars

¿Dónde está el cajero automático más cercano? - Where's the nearest cash machine?

Perdí mi tarjeta de banco - I've lost my bank card

Quiero informar de… - I want to report a…

una tarjeta de crédito perdida - lost credit card

una tarjeta de crédito robada - stolen credit card

He olvidado mi contraseña de banco en línea - I've forgotten my Internet banking password

He olvidado mi número de PIN - I've forgotten my PIN number

ATM

Inserte su tarjeta - Insert your card

Ingrese su número de PIN - Enter your PIN

PIN incorrecto - Incorrect PIN

Ingresar - Enter

Correcto - Correct

Cancelar - Cancel

Retirar dinero - Withdraw cash

Otra cantidad - Other amount

Por favor, espere - Please wait

Fondos insuficientes - Insufficient funds

Saldo - Balance

Impreso - Printed

¿Desea un recibo? - Would you like a receipt?

Retirar tarjeta - Remove card

Salir - Quit

Important terms

portátil - laptop

tableta digital - tablet

pantalla - screen

teclado - keyboard

impresora - printer

cable - cord

disco duro - hard drive

altavoces - speakers

cable de alimentación - power cord

correo electrónico/email - email

aplicación - app

cargador - phone charger

dirección de correo electrónico - email address

usuario - username

contraseña - password

responder - to reply

reenviar - to forward

nuevo mensaje - new message

archivo adjunto - attachment

enchufar - to plug in

desenchufar - to unplug

encender - to switch on

apagar - to switch off

reiniciar - to restart

internet - Internet

sitio web - website

wifi - WiFi

descargar - to download

archivo - file

carpeta - folder

documento - document

iniciar sesión - to log in

cerrar sesión - to log out

memoria - memory

imprimir - to print

Chapter 14 - Spare Time

When visiting the theater, museum or club, these phrases may help you:

Theatre

¿Hay algo en el teatro…? - Is there anything on at the theatre…?

esta noche - tonight

esta semana - this week

este mes - this month

¿Hasta cuándo está la obra? - When's the play on until?

¿Quién actúa? - Who's in it?

¿Qué tipo de producción es? - What type of production is it?

Es… - It's…

una comedia - a comedy

una tragedia - a tragedy

un musical - a musical

una ópera - an opera

un ballet - a ballet

¿La has visto antes? - Have you seen it before?

¿A qué hora comienza el espectáculo? - What time does the performance start?

¿A qué hora termina? - What time does it finish?

¿Dónde está el guardarropa? - Where's the cloakroom?

¿Desea un programa? - Would you like a program?

¿Puede darme un programa, por favor? - Could I have a program, please?

¿Pedimos algo de beber para el entreacto? - Shall we order some drinks for the interval?

Deberíamos volver a nuestros asientos - We'd better go back to our seats

¿Te ha gustado? - Did you enjoy it?

The club

¿Quieres ir a un club/una discoteca esta noche? - Do you want to go to a club tonight?

¿Hay alguna buena discoteca en esta zona? - Do you know any good clubs near here?

¿Hasta qué hora abre? - Until what time is it open?

¿A qué hora cierran? - What time does it close?

¿Cuánto cuesta la entrada? - How much is it to get in?

¿Hay un código de vestimenta? - Is there a dress code?

¿Qué noches abren? - What nights are you open?

¿Qué tipo de música es? - What sort of music is it?

¿Qué hay esta noche? - What's on tonight?

¿Hay música en vivo esta noche? - Is there any live music tonight?

Disculpe, no puede entrar - Sorry, you can't come in

No puede entrar con zapatillas - You can't come in with trainers on

Hay una fiesta privada esta noche - There's a private party tonight

El club está lleno - The club's full

Estoy en la lista de invitados - I'm on the guest list

Soy miembro - I'm a member

¿Dónde está el guardarropa? - Where's the cloakroom?

¿Qué piensas del DJ? - What do you think of the DJ?

¡La música es genial! - The music's great!

Está un poco vacío - It's a bit empty

¿Dónde está el bar? - Where's the bar?

Hay una larga fila en el bar - There's a long queue at the bar

Está demasiado ruidoso - It's too loud

Hace demasiado calor aquí - It's too hot in here

¿Estás listo/a para ir a casa? - Are you ready to go home?

Me voy a casa - I'm going home

Flirting - Small Talk

¿Puedo comprarte algo de beber? - May I buy you something to drink?

¿Vienes aquí a menudo? - Do you come here often?

¿En qué trabajas? - So, what do you do for a living?

¿Quieres bailar? - Do you want to dance?

¿Quieres tomar aire fresco? - Would you like to get some fresh air?

¿Quieres ir a otra fiesta? - Do you want to go to a different party?

¡Vayámonos de aquí! - Let's get out of here!

¿Mi casa o tu casa? - My place or yours?

¿Quieres ver una película en mi casa? - Would you like to watch a movie at my place?

¿Tienes planes para esta noche? - Do you have any plans for tonight?

¿Te gustaría comer conmigo uno de estos días? - Would you like to eat with me sometime?

¿Quieres ir a tomar un café? - Would you like to go get a coffee?

¿Puedo acompañarte/llevarte a tu casa? - May I walk/drive you home?

¿Quieres que nos volvamos a ver? - Would you like to meet again?

¡Gracias por una hermosa noche! - Thank you for a lovely evening!

¿Quieres entrar y tomar una taza de café? - Would you like to come inside for a coffee?

¡Eres hermoso/a! - You're gorgeous!

¡Eres gracioso/a! - You're funny!

¡Tienes unos ojos hermosos! - You have beautiful eyes!

¡Bailas muy bien! - You're a great dancer!

¡He estado pensando en ti todo el día! - I have been thinking about you all day!

¡Ha sido muy agradable charlar contigo! - It's been really nice talking to you!

No estoy interesado/a - I'm not interested

Déjame solo/a - Leave me alone

¡Piérdete! - Get lost!

¡No me toques! - Don't touch me!

¡Quítame las manos de encima! - Get your hands off me!

Museum and Gallery

¿Cuánto cuesta la entrada? - How much is it to get in?

¿Hay un precio de admisión? - Is there an admission charge?

Solo para la exhibición - Only for the exhibition

¿A qué hora cierran? - What time do you close?

El museo cierra los lunes - The museum's closed on Mondays

¿Puedo tomar fotografías? - Can I take photographs?

¿Le gustaría una audioguía? - Would you like an audio-guide?

¿Hay visitas guiadas en el día de hoy? - Are there any guided tours today?

¿A qué hora comienza la próxima visita guiada? - What time does the next guided tour start?

¿Dónde está el guardarropa? - Where's the cloakroom?

Tenemos que dejar nuestros bolsos en el guardarropa - We have to leave our bags in the cloakroom

¿Tiene un plano del museo? - Do you have a plan of the museum?

¿Quién pintó este cuadro? - Who's this painting by?

Este museo tiene una buena colección de… - This museum's got a very good collection of…

pinturas al óleo - oil paintings

acuarelas - watercolours

retratos - portraits

paisajes - landscapes

esculturas - sculptures

artefactos antiguos - ancient artifacts

cerámica - pottery

¿Te gusta…? - do you like…?

el arte moderno - modern art

las pinturas clásicas - classical paintings

las pinturas impresionistas - impressionist paintings

Important terms

plaza - square

parque - park

calle - street

panadería/pastelería - bakery

tienda de libros/librería - bookshop

tienda de ropa - clothes shop

floristería - florists

tienda de regalos - gift shop

juguetería - toy shop

galería de arte - art gallery

banco - bank

bar - bar

cafetería - café

catedral - cathedral

iglesia - church

cine - cinema

sala de conciertos - concert hall

gimnasio - gym

biblioteca - library

museo - museum

centro comercial - shopping centre

teatro - theatre

cementerio - cemetery

mercado - marketplace

estadio - stadium

zoológico - zoo

ruinas - ruins

Chapter 15 - Useful words and terms

Here are some useful words and their translation so you can quickly express your thoughts:

Landscape and geographical terms

campo - countryside

colina - hill

montaña - mountain

valle - valley

madera - wood

bosque - forest

campo - field

selva/jungla - jungle

sendero - path

cerca - fence

muro - wall

granja - farm

puente - bridge

desierto - desert

glaciar - glacier

volcán - volcano

río - river

canal - canal

lago - lake

cascada - waterfall

mina - mine

ganado - livestock

cosechar - to harvest

océano - ocean

mar - sea

playa - beach

isla - island

ola - wave

faro - lighthouse

país - country

ciudad - city

pueblo - town

terremoto - earthquake

frontera - border

parque nacional - national park

medioambiente - environment

paisaje - landscape

urbano - urban

rural - rural

The weather

Sol - sun

sol - sunshine

lluvia - rain

nieve - snow

granizo - hail

llovizna - drizzle

neblina - mist

niebla - fog

nube - cloud

arcoiris - rainbow

viento - wind

brisa - breeze

trueno - thunder

relámpago - lightning

tormenta - storm

huracán - hurricane

inundación - flood

helada - frost

hielo - ice

ventoso - windy

nublado - cloudy

seco - dry

húmedo - humid

calor - heat

frío - cold

soleado - sunny

lluvioso - rainy

nevar - to snow

llover - to rain

pronóstico del tiempo - weather forecast

temperatura - temperature

alta presión - high pressure

baja presión - low pressure

barómetro - barometer

grado - degree

centígrado/Celsius - Celsius

Home appliances

baterías/pilas - battery

velas - candles

algodón - cotton

pegamento - glue

bombilla - light bulb

mechero - lighter

fósforos/cerillas - matches

aguja - needle

tijeras - scissors

bolígrafo/pluma - pen

lápiz - pencil

pañuelos - tissues

papel higiénico - toilet paper

jabón/detergente - detergent

jabón para lavar la ropa - washing powder

Animals

perro - dog

gato - cat

conejo - rabbit

vaca/res - cow

oveja/cordero - sheep

cerdo/puerco - pig

caballo - horse

pollo - chicken

ratón - mouse

rata - rat

sapo - frog

serpiente/víbora - snake

león - lion

tigre - tiger

mono - monkey

elefante - elephant

jirafa - giraffe

oso - bear

paloma - pigeon

águila - eagle

hormiga - ant

mosca - fly

mosquito - mosquito

araña - spider

abeja - bee

avispa - wasp

mariposa - butterfly

trucha - trout

salmón - salmon

atún - tuna

cangrejo - crab

Useful adjectives

grande - big

pequeño - small

rápido - fast

lento - slow

bueno - good

malo - bad

caro - expensive

barato - cheap

grueso - thick

fino - thin

estrecho - narrow

ancho - wide

ruidoso - loud

silencioso - quiet

inteligente - intelligent

estúpido - stupid

mojado - wet

seco - dry

pesado - heavy

liviano - light

duro - hard

suave - soft

fácil - easy

difícil - difficult

débil - weak

fuerte - strong

rico - rich

pobre - poor

joven - young

viejo - old

largo - long

corto - short

alto - high

bajo - low

generoso - generous

malvado - mean

verdadero - true

falso - false

bello - beautiful

feo - ugly

nuevo - new

viejo - old

feliz/alegre - happy

triste - sad

seguro - safe

peligroso - dangerous

temprano - early

tarde - late

abierto - open

cerrado - closed

lleno - full

vacío - empty

muchos - many

pocos - few

interesante - interesting

aburrido - boring

importante - important

sin importancia - unimportant

correcto - right

incorrecto - wrong

lejos - far

cerca - near

limpio - clean

sucio - dirty

agradable - pleasant

desagradable - unpleasant

excelente - excellent

terrible - terrible

justo - fair

injusto - unfair

normal - normal

anormal - abnormal

Chapter 16 - Tips for learning a new language

Are you in the middle of planning your trip? Did you think of everything? First aid kit, papers & documents? Very good, but what about your foreign language skills? Have you ever thought of how you'll express yourself? Unfortunately, many travelers neglect this topic and think that with English you can get anywhere. And some also assume that you can communicate well with your hands and feet. The question that you should ask yourself is:

What do I expect from my journey and which goal do I have?

To give you a little motivation, here are 5 advantages of being able to express yourself in a foreign language:

 - You get to know the locals much more authentically

 - You understand the culture and attitude of people much better

 - You can negotiate more effectively

 - You do not waste valuable time, because you understand faster

 - You feel safer

Just to keep it short: You do not have to learn the foreign language to perfection. But you should be able to communicate properly. Here are some tips on how to learn certain basics quickly and effectively.

Are you ready? Okay, then we can start. Depending on how much time you have until the trip, you should use the time well. Which language level you achieve depends entirely on you. Here are some essential recommendations on how to learn a language.

1. Speak from the first day

Unfortunately, many people follow a wrong approach when learning a language. A language is a means of communication and should therefore be lived rather than learned. There is no such thing as an "I am ready now." Therefore, just jump into the cold water and speak already at home from the first day on. That sounds horrible and silly? It does not matter how it sounds, with time it will get better. It is best to set the goal not to miss a day when you have not used the foreign language in any form. Just try to implement everything you learn directly. So speak, write and think in your foreign language.

2. Immerse yourself in the foreign language at home

This tip actually goes hand in hand with the first recommendation. To learn the foreign language quickly and efficiently, you have to integrate it firmly into your everyday life. It is not enough if you learn a few words from time to time and engage in grammar and pronunciation. This has to be done much more intensively. You have to dive properly into the foreign language. Just bring foreign countries to your home. By the so-called "immersion" you surround yourself almost constantly and everywhere with the learning language.

3. Change the language setting on devices

For example, you could change the menu language of your smartphone or laptop from your native language to your learning language. Since you use your smartphone or your laptop every day, you know where to find something and learn some vocabulary along the way. Of course you can also do the same with your social networks like Facebook and Twitter. But watch out that you are always able to change back the menu language!

4. Use foreign language media

You could, for example, get a foreign language newspaper. If that is not available or too expensive, then there are enough newspapers or news portals where you can read news online. Probably you are already familiar with the news through your native language, then the context is easier if you read the same messages again in the foreign language. Further aids are foreign-language films or series. It's probably best to start with a movie or series that you've already seen in your native language. The slang and common phrases can make it really hard for you. If you realize that you are not understanding it well, try the subtitle in the foreign language. If that does not work, then take the subtitle of your native language and try again. Even music should not be neglected in your foreign-language world. This has the advantage of teaching you a lot about the pronunciation and emphasis. Incidentally, you are getting a lot closer to the culture of the country.

5. Set notes in your apartment

If it does not bother you and others, spread little sticky notes with words in the apartment. Whether this is your toothbrush, the couch or the remote control, just place notes on as many objects and pieces of furniture as possible with the respective name of the object in the foreign language. As a result, you have the vocabulary all day long and memorize it automatically.

6. Learn the most important phrases

Another helpful tip is to think about what words and phrases you'll need before you travel. For example, you could write down how to reserve a hotel room or book a bus ride. Even how to order in the restaurant, ask someone for directions and how to communicate with the doctor or the police. Of course, this book is more than enough and you have all the phrases at one place.

7. Set clear goals

Last but not least, an important piece of advice: Set clear goals. Without goals, you will never get where you want to go. Since you have already booked your flight, you also have a deadline, to which you have reached a goal you have set. To accomplish this, you can now place mini orders. But stay realistic with your goals, especially in relation to your mini goals. If they are too big and not realistically achievable, you may lose your courage and give up. A good tip is also that you record your goals in writing because writing is like having a contract with yourself. It makes your goals more binding and makes you feel more obligated to stick to your schedule. The writing down also has the advantage that you have to formulate your goals more precisely and not forget them so quickly. Do not just try to formulate these goals, but really approach them and implement them

Here are some examples of how you could define your goals:

- Learn 300 words
- Memorize 5 phrases
- Write an email in the foreign language
- Memorize important questions
- Conduct a talk online via webcam

How can you achieve your goals?

- Set Priorities: Be sure to rank your goals by importance!
- Stay realistic: What is your current life situation?
- Start today: Do not think about tomorrow or yesterday, but start today to reach your goals! The longer you wait, the less likely you are to achieve your goals
- Tell others about it: If others know about your goals, then you will do everything possible to reach them. Otherwise, you would have to admit defeat. This tip could of course make you stress, but will help you to work purposefully!
- Change your habits: You may need to change something in your daily routine to achieve your goals. Do not hesitate and reject bad habits that get in your way!
- Reward yourself: Every time you reach a partial goal, do something good! You know best what that can be!
- Obviously, you do not have to punish yourself, but some people are more likely to do it than to be rewarded for success

- Let the imagination play: Imagine how it is when you reach your goals. What would you be capable of? What would you feel? This will motivate you immensely to work on your goals!

8. Humor

Do not feel sad if it does not work right away. You may be embarrassing yourself in front of a native speaker because you mispronounce a word and make a completely different sense. Nobody will blame you. For most people it means a lot that you try to learn their language. And when they laugh then they do not mean that. But the most important thing is: have fun getting to know a new language! After all, you do not have any pressure, as you do at school.

Mastering the foreign language of your destination country has only advantages. You will learn to understand how people of a particular region think, what fears and worries they have and how they tackle life. You'll become more tolerant and see the world differently and, after your journey, you'll definitely question many ways of thinking of your own culture. Of course, you will also learn a lot of new things abroad, even in foreign languages. But please take the time already and get familiar with the new language before you leave. We promise you, it's worth it!

Conclusion

¡Hola nuevamente!

We really hope you enjoyed our Spanish phrase book for beginners!

Now, no matter where you are in Latin America or Spain, you'll carry with you the essentials to carry out a basic conversation, get out of trouble, shop, make friends, introduce yourself and much more.

We dare you to challenge yourself and explore Spanish even further, until this book is no longer necessary for you. Read short stories in Spanish, novels, newspapers, websites, watch films and immerse yourself in as many Spanish-speaking countries as you can.

Try every possible food and learn its ingredients and recipe. Ask locals about their slang, their local dishes and customs. Not only will you end up being absolutely fluent in Spanish, but also you'll make tons of new friends and you'll get to know a lot about the world and different cultures. This will definitely make you feel a richer person.

So, if this is nothing but a starting point, we hope it was useful for you to take your first steps into this amazing, complex, ever-changing language.

¡Buena suerte!

If you enjoyed this book, can you please leave a review for it?

Thanks for your support!